NPL|F
Nashville Public Library | FOUNDATION

The **Middle School Rules** of

CHARLES TILLMAN "Peanut"

as told by Sean Jensen

Illustrated by Max Smith

BroadStreet
PUBLISHING

BroadStreet Publishing Group LLC
Racine, Wisconsin, USAwww.broadstreetpublishing.com

Middle School Rules of Charles Tillman

ISBN 978-1-4245-5101-9 (hard cover)
ISBN 978-1-4245-5102-6 (e-book)

Illustrated by Max Smith | maxsmithdraws.com
Cover and interior design by Garborg Design Works | garborgdesign.com
Editorial services provided by Ginger Garrett | gingergarrett.com
and Michelle Winger | literallyprecise.com

Printed in China.

15 16 17 18 19 20 21   7 6 5 4 3 2 1

ACKNOWLEDGMENTS

from Charles Tillman

I want to thank my Lord and Savior, Jesus Christ, for
giving me my talent and placing the right people in my life
to get me to where I am today.
Thank you to the entire Tillman family for always believing in me
and all my friends who have—and continue to be—close allies.
A special thank you to my beautiful wife Jackie for supporting me
and pushing me to my maximum potential, especially off the field.
To Tayla, Tiana, Tysen, and Tessa: You inspire me to be better and
do better by you and for you.

from Sean Jensen

First and foremost, all glory to God,
for his enduring love and grace.
Thanks to my parents for pushing and raising me.
Special thanks to my wife Erica for challenging me
to become the man God designed me to be—
and always supporting me along the way.
Lastly, thank God for my son Elijah and daughter Zarah for
entertaining me, humbling me, and inspiring me.

INTRODUCTION

Dear Reader

I'm very excited about the *Middle School Rules* series.

I wasn't always the biggest, the fastest, or the smartest growing up. I was actually quite small, hence the nickname *Peanut*.

My experiences growing up molded me and helped me become the man I am today. I made many mistakes and suffered some setbacks, but I always searched for the lessons.

I'm not that different from you all, as you will see in this book. I faced some of the same challenges that you may be dealing with. Not *if*, but *when* you have trials, my hope is that you can rely on some of my rules to guide you through your struggle.

Some of my closest friends don't even know some of these defining childhood stories, but I wanted to share them with you. I hope you can relate to me and learn something, so you can overcome your challenge and reflect proudly on how you handled it.

These rules aren't just meant to be for this book. They are also instilled in my own children.

I was blessed to have two wonderful parents, who did an amazing job of raising me and teaching me right from wrong. But I've also been extremely blessed to have so many other relatives, mentors, and friends who have helped me along the way.

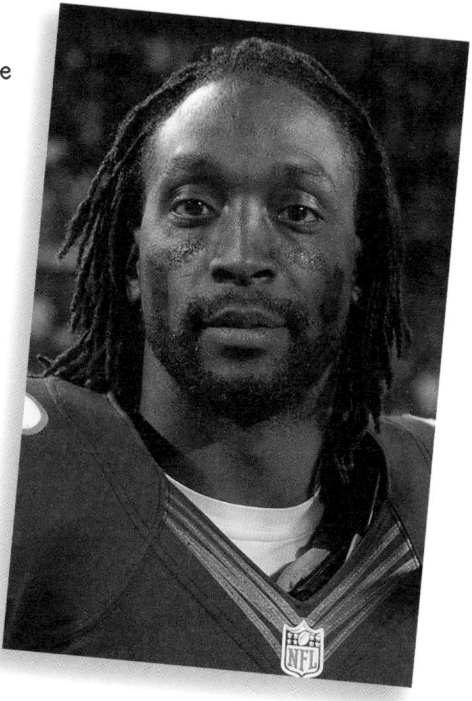

Guidance doesn't always come from family. It can come from many sources, and I encourage you to be on the lookout for the people who want to have a positive influence in your life.

Be blessed,

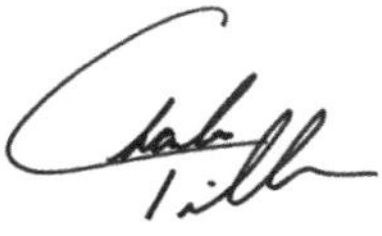

Charles Tillman

FOREWORD

On a sunny day in June 2003, Charles "Peanut" Tillman walked into our home and into our hearts. My wife, Deanna, and I were running a leadership and life skills camp for the Chicago Bears' 2003 rookie class. Within 24 hours of getting to know Peanut, Deanna turned to me and proclaimed, "He is going to be a superstar in the NFL."

I laughed that off. "How on earth can you tell?"

She replied, "Trust me. I can tell."

Well, she was right. Peanut has not only become a superstar in the NFL, but a superstar in life.

Many athletes struggle after their professional playing career ends. I was fortunate. I was an All American for my athletic and academic success at the University of Illinois, where I left as the school's all-time leading receiver. Like Peanut, I was selected in the second round, though I started my NFL career with the Atlanta Falcons. After being traded to the Detroit Lions, I suffered a severe Achilles injury during my third season. But my story was only beginning.

I've spent 40 years in the financial services business, recruiting, training, and developing the most field management leaders in the history of Northwestern Mutual. I'm a national speaker, voted Best Speaker at the NFL Rookie Symposium six times.

I've met many great men in my life, but Peanut is one of the most remarkable. In this book, you'll see Peanut's *grit*, a word that reflects work ethic but also toughness. What makes Peanut truly special is that he combines grit with *zest*: a charisma and love for life.

Most people who become successful in life had a role model: someone they looked up to, respected, and learned from. Peanut had many successful men and women in his life that he listened to. They helped him become the man he is today. *The Middle School Rules of Charles Tillman* is a book about Peanut's life. But it is also a book that you can learn from. It can make Peanut one of *your* mentors.

Don't just read this book... study it.

John Wright
CEO Wright Financial Group, Inc.

TABLE OF CONTENTS

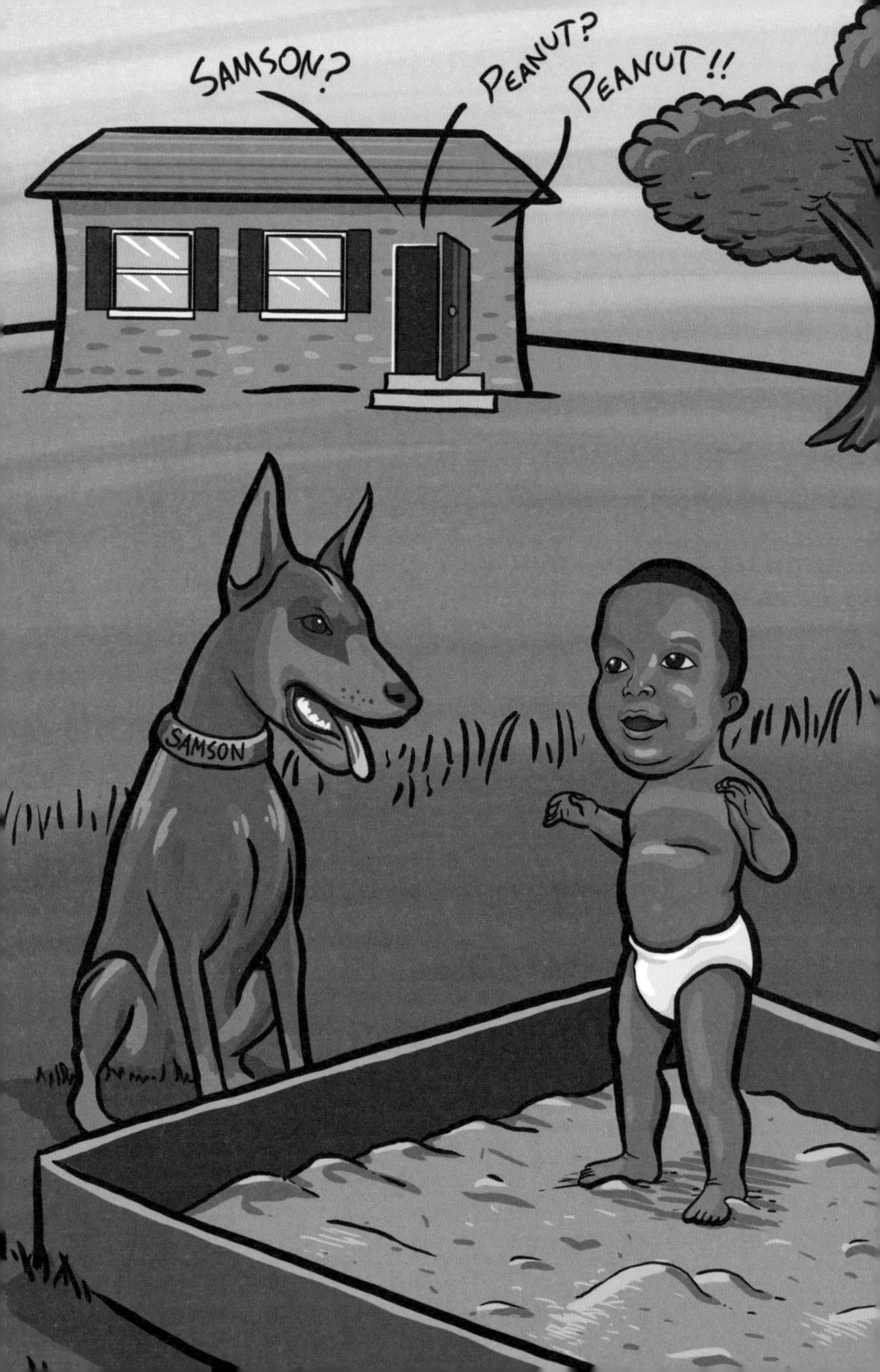
SAMSON?
PEANUT?
PEANUT!!
SAMSON

Chapter 1 Peanut's Family

Rule: Respect, Respect, Respect

Chicago boasts one of the finest skylines in the world. Everywhere you look, beautiful buildings rise high into the sky, including the famous 102-story Sears Tower (most recently called the Willis Tower). But in late February 1981, a heavy fog swallowed the city. If you stood outside, you could barely see across the street.

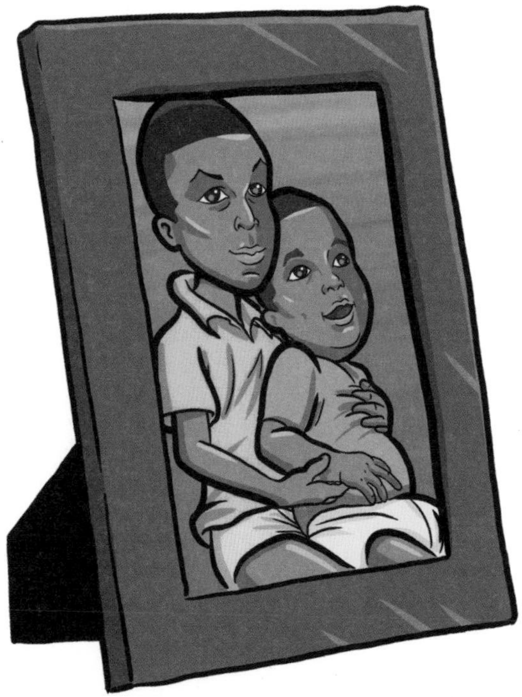

In that cold, foggy weather, on February 23rd, Charles Anthony Tillman was born, at the University of Chicago Medical Center on 59th Street and Cottage Grove Avenue. Then the fog lifted, and the temperature soared—all the way to the mid-50s.

That's *really* warm for a Chicago winter day.

Weighing 6 pounds, 15 ounces at birth, he was the second child—and second boy—born to Tiny and Lil' Donald Tillman.

Charles had chubby cheeks and big, bright eyes: traits Aunt Renee shared with him.

But the first time she saw him, Aunt Renee noticed a slight point at the top of his head, which is common for newborns. She said with a grin, "Look at that little peanut-headed boy." And that's how Charles got his nickname: Peanut.

Many of Peanut's relatives had nicknames:

Tiny or Momma: Mom—Arbria. She was small!

Lil' Donald or Deddy: Dad—but his real name was Donald Jr. He was big!

Duck: Brother—Donald (after the famous Disney duck)

Gummy Bear or Granddeddy: Grandfather—Donald Sr.

Pooh: Aunt—Prudence

Lieutenant Dan: Aunt—Renee (after the character in the movie *Forrest Gump*)

Bev: Aunt—Beverly

As Peanut grew, he was always smiling and showing off his deep dimples. He was constantly on the move too, searching for new adventures. He found plenty, especially when his family moved to Louisiana. Peanut was two years old.

Just after lunch one day, Tiny called her husband. She was very upset.

"Peanut is gone! Peanut is gone!"

Lil' Donald rushed home. He quickly realized that the family's red Doberman Pinscher, Samson, was also missing.

"Peanut! Samson! Where are you?" he yelled.

Tiny and Lil' Donald searched throughout the house, peeking under beds, throwing open closets, and even looking behind curtains.

Then Lil' Donald had a thought. *Could Peanut be outside?*

That didn't seem possible. Could he have escaped the house and taken the dog for an adventure? Just in case, Lil' Donald opened the back door and walked outside. At the bottom of the sloping hill in their backyard, there was a sandbox. Lil' Donald watched as Peanut gleefully tossed sand up into the air while Samson dutifully sat just two feet away in the grass.

Lil' Donald didn't get mad. He was surprised. Peanut was still in diapers, after all. But as Peanut got older, Lil' Donald started to yell his real name more often. When Peanut was in trouble, he would hear, "Charles Anthony Tillman!"

Peanut and Duck called their father *Deddy*, which sort of sounds like *Daddy*. Deddy had strict rules, and Peanut sometimes broke them.

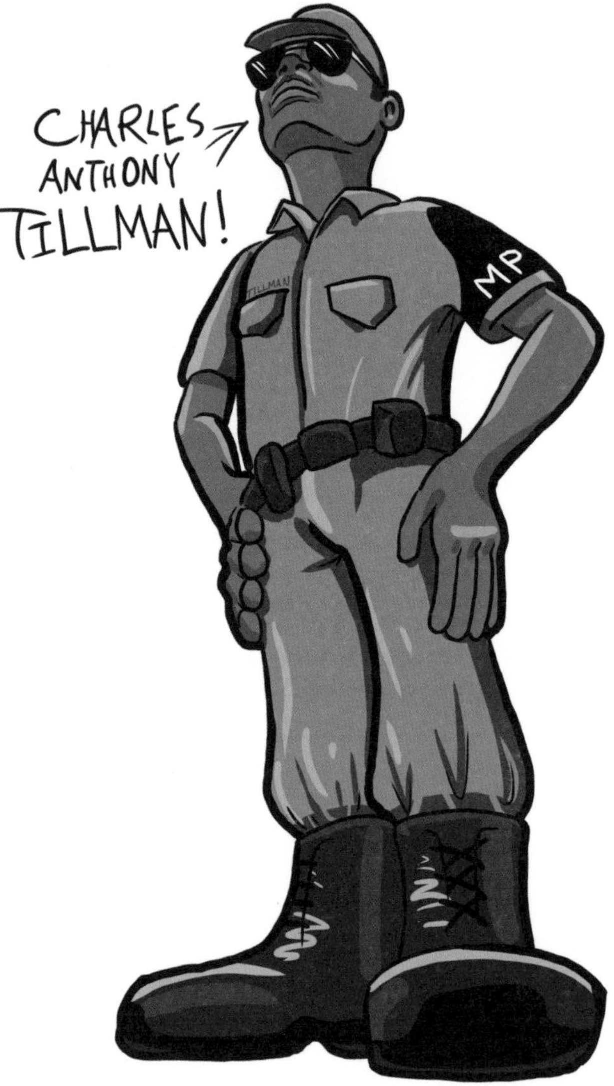
CHARLES
ANTHONY
TILLMAN!
TILLMAN
MP

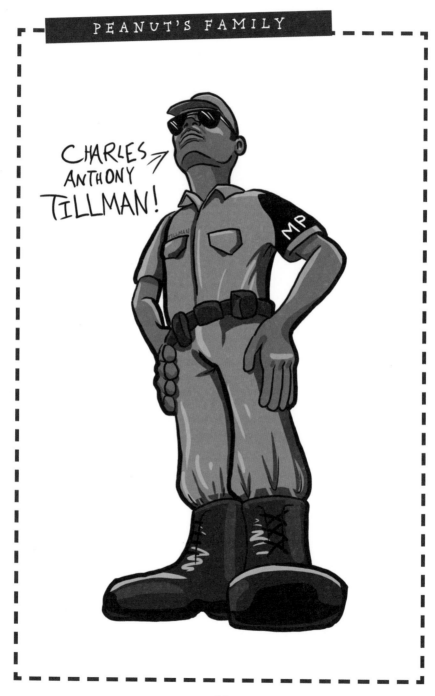

<u>Deddy and Momma's Rules</u>

Lil' Donald was in the Army. He expected his children to obey the rules, which included

1. Honor your elders and address them with respect, meaning no bad attitudes, and do not reply with "Huh?" or "What?"

2. Speak clearly and properly, without slang.

"Me and Duck are figuring to..." Peanut once began.

"What did you say?" Deddy firmly asked.

"I mean, Duck and I..."

3. Open doors for ladies.

4. Say, "Thank you" whenever appropriate.

Peanut quickly learned that if he was in trouble, obeying rule number one was always a good idea.

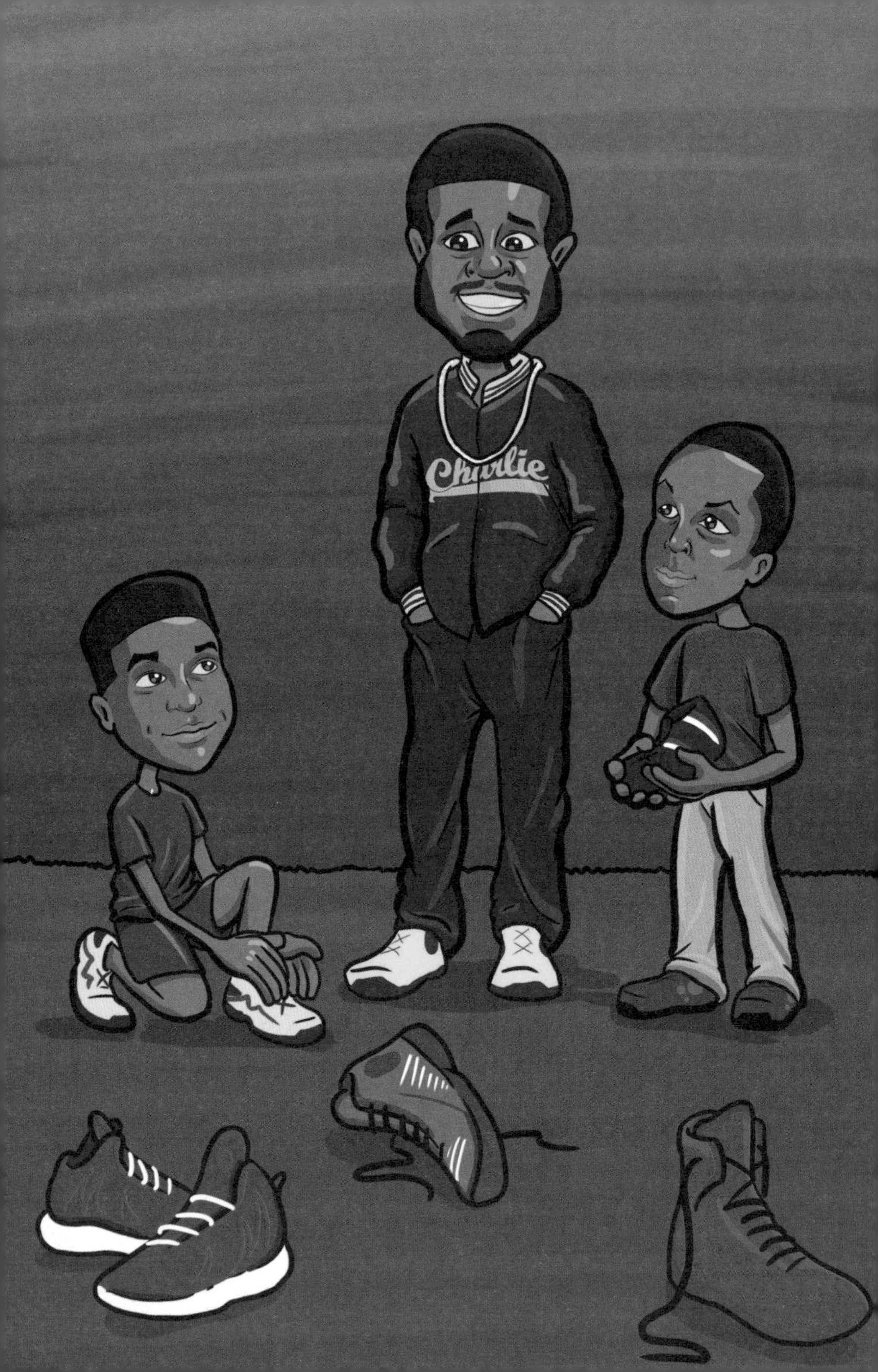
Charlie

Chapter 2

Family Matters

Rule: Look Out for Each Other

Peanut's grandparents worked hard to keep the family close—and food was the key.

Granddeddy specialized in cooking breakfast, and he always made way too much. Peanut and his brother Duck didn't complain though!

Granddeddy's Breakfast Menu

Pancakes
Homemade hash browns
Grits
Bacon
Sausage
Eggs—any way you want them

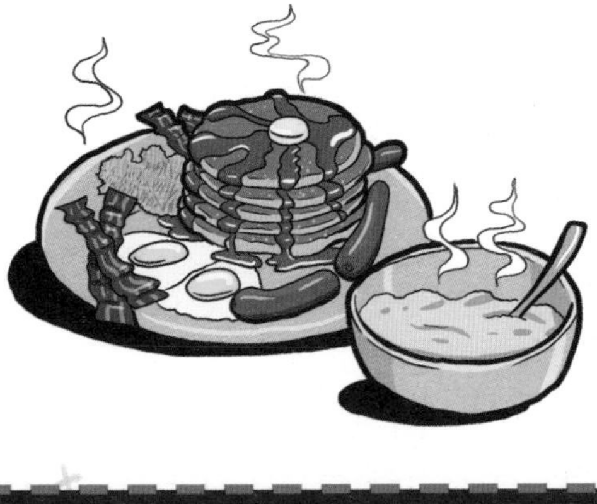

Everyone in the family was a great cook. Grandma Alice, who was Lil' Donald's mother, made the best dinner rolls, with just enough butter, and her Red

Velvet cake was a family favorite. Cousins, aunts, and uncles would gather for cookouts and delicious fish fries. The family loved good food *and* good music. Grandma Alice adored dancing to The Temptations, The O'Jays, and Marvin Gaye, which all had popular music hits at the time.

Peanut and his cousins would make up dance routines too. Other times, they would play tag in the yard.

Peanut and Duck really liked the family gatherings because they didn't always get to hang out with their extended family. Lil' Donald was in the Army, so the family had to move often, usually every couple of years. Family time was special, especially when Uncle Charlie, which everyone pronounced *Cholly*, was there. He was the youngest of the aunts and uncles—and he was the coolest.

Each time Peanut's family would return to Chicago, Uncle Charlie would take Peanut and Duck on a shopping trip. He spoiled them! Whatever the hottest shoe was at the time—whether it was Jordan, Fila, Reebok, or adidas—Uncle Charlie bought a pair for each boy. Uncle Charlie loved shoes. He had the biggest shoe collection the boys had ever seen, and he wore lots of gold jewelry.

After the shopping spree, Uncle Charlie would give each of the boys $40.

"Thanks, Uncle Charlie!" Peanut and Duck would say.

When Uncle Charlie would see his buddies or acquaintances, he would say, "These are my nephews."

Time with Uncle Charlie was a rare treat though. The boys spent most of their time with their aunts Prudence and Renee.

Peanut and Duck jokingly called Aunt Renee *Lieutenant Dan,* after the tough and strict character in the movie *Forrest Gump.* Aunt Renee always insisted everything be clean and in order. If the boys misbehaved, she disciplined them.

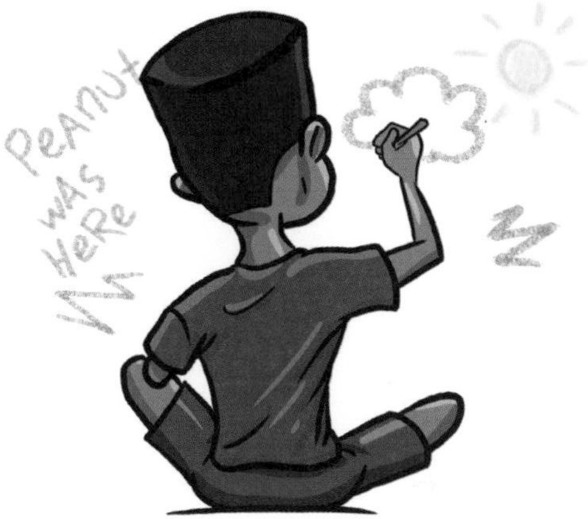
PEANUT WAS HERE

Once, Peanut scribbled on her wall with crayons, and she made him scrub it all off.

"You're always making us clean something," Peanut protested, though not loud enough for Aunt Renee to actually hear him. He knew that defiant disrespect would get him a *whooping* (another term for a spanking). Deddy's rule was an important one, but Aunt Prudence had a few of her own too.

The boys didn't grow up attending church, but they always had to when they stayed with most of their aunties, especially Aunt Prudence. That was her first rule. Peanut remembered Deddy's number one rule to always honor his elders and treat them with respect.

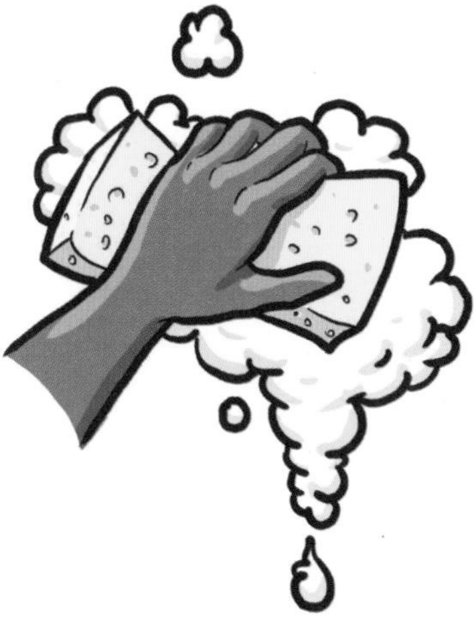

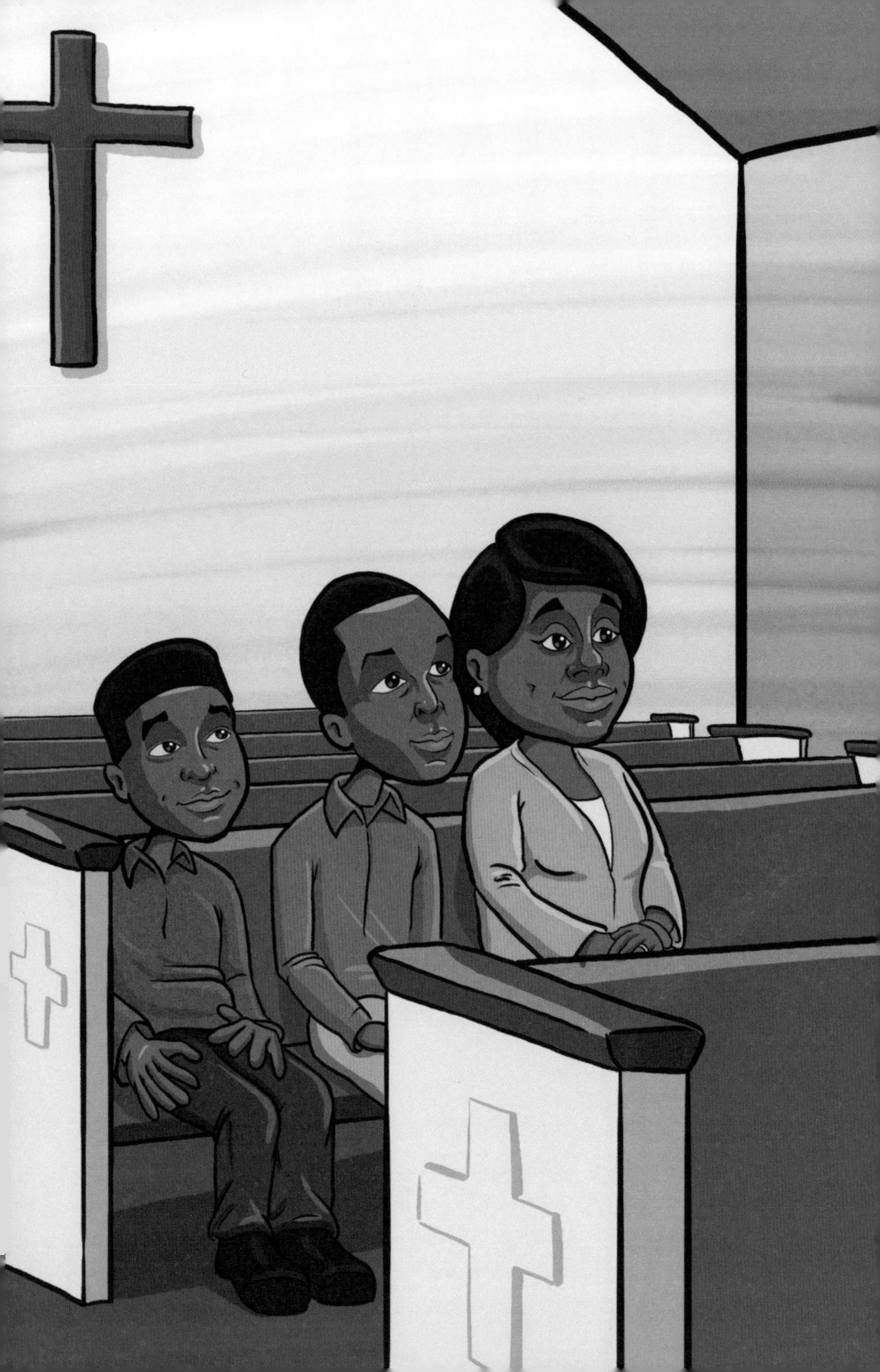

Chapter 3 Peanut Goes to Church

Aunt Prudence's Rule

"If you can be out and about with your friends and stay out late on Saturday, and the Lord has blessed you to wake up on Sunday," Aunt Prudence said, "then you can give him some time."

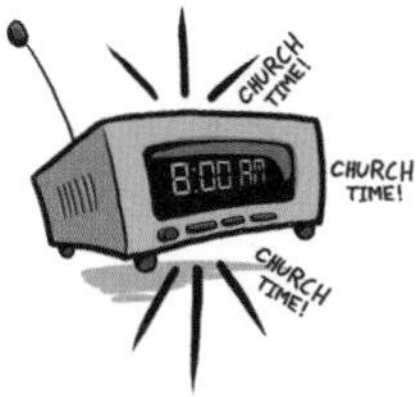
CHURCH TIME!
8:00 AM
CHURCH TIME!
CHURCH TIME!

This rule meant there was no sleeping in on Sundays at Aunt Prudence's. She would go through the house, wake everyone up, and make them put on nice church clothes.

The church service started at 8 a.m. sharp!

The wooden Southern Baptist church in Texas wasn't air conditioned, and the members clapped and danced and belted out old Gospel hymns. Brother Sercy was the pastor.

When Brother Sercy would get into a groove during his sermon, Aunt Prudence would be among the most outspoken in the congregation, offering him encouragement.

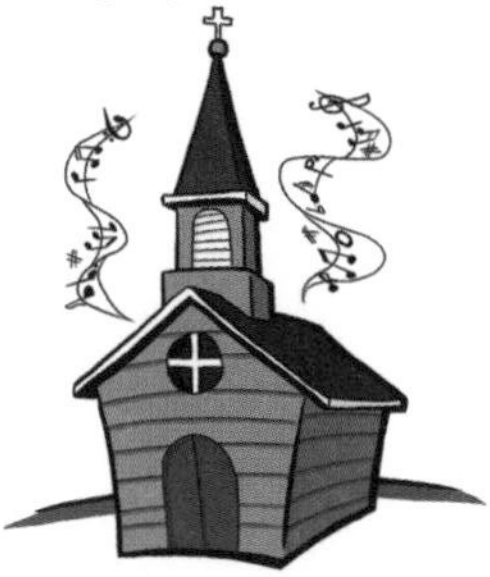

"All right, Brother Sercy," she'd say. "Preach now!"

Aunt Prudence also liked to take the boys to church on Wednesday nights for Bible study. They liked watching cartoon tales of Noah and Jonah and the real purpose of Easter.

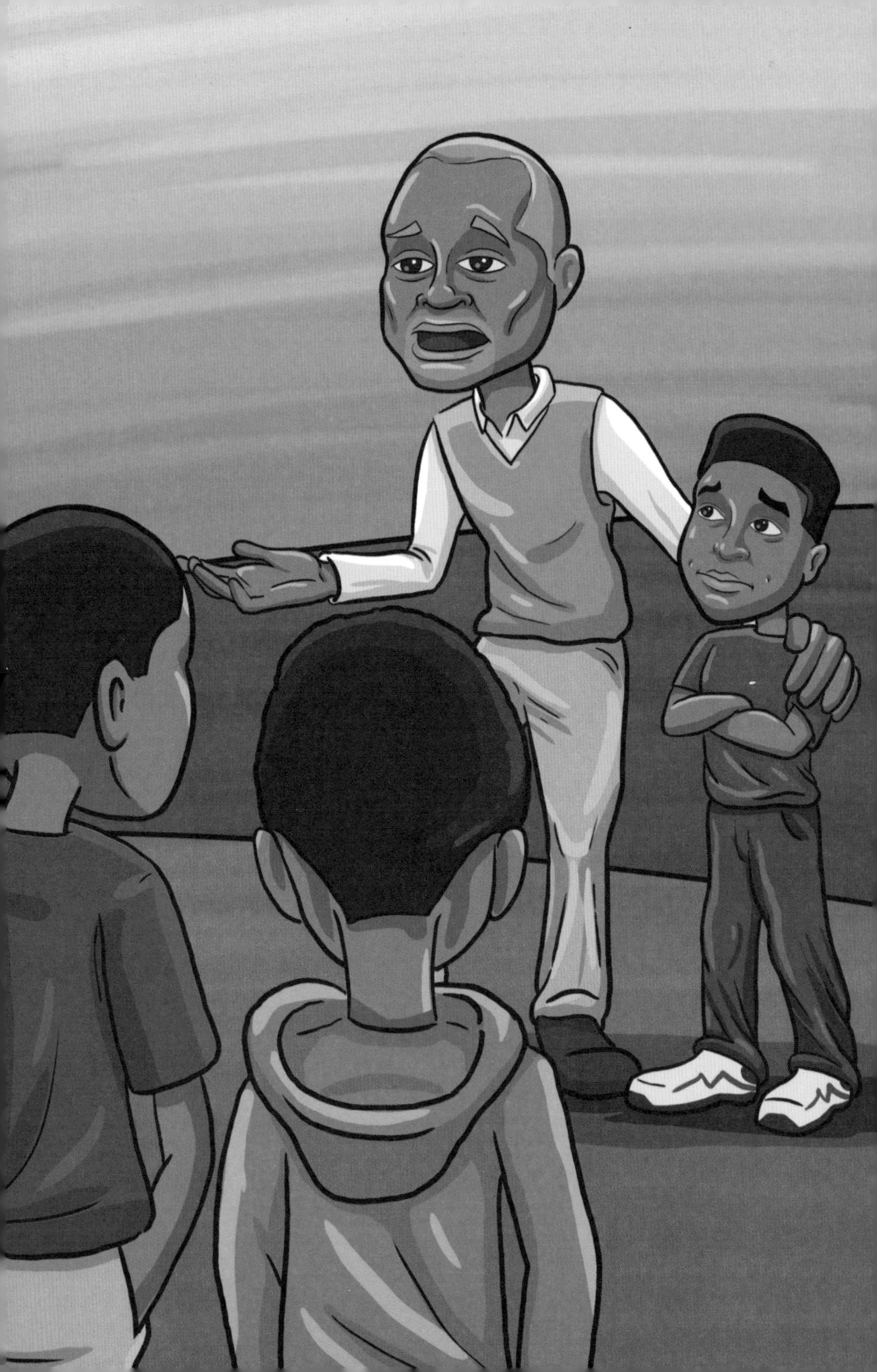

Chapter 4 Stick Together

Peanut and Duck respected their Deddy, but they feared Granddeddy.

One summer, when Peanut was five years old, he and Duck were staying with Granddeddy and Grandma Jean. Along with Cousin Mike, the boys walked to a friend's house in the neighborhood one bright morning. Their friend's name was Barry. Barry let Duck and Cousin Mike in, but he refused to let Peanut come in. Barry said Peanut was annoying.

"You always get on my nerves!" Barry said and slammed the door in Peanut's face.

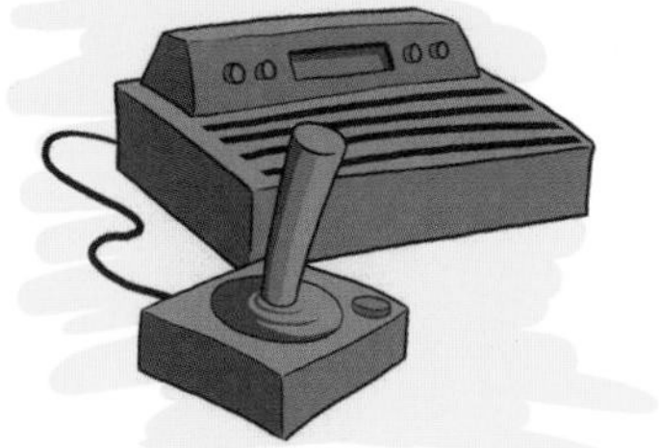

Peanut hung his head. He knew Duck would stay at Barry's house, just for the chance to play video games. Barry had a cool game system.

Peanut walked back to his Granddeddy's house on South Paxton Avenue in Chicago all alone.

"Where is everyone?" Granddeddy asked Peanut.

"They're at Barry's house," Peanut said, trying not to sound sad or jealous.

"Why you ain't there?" Granddeddy asked.

Peanut swallowed nervously. He didn't want to get Duck in

trouble. "They said I couldn't go in." Peanut didn't blame anyone by name.

Granddeddy frowned. He grabbed his keys and told Peanut to get into the van. They drove in silence the few blocks to Barry's house.

Peanut's eyes grew wide as Granddeddy banged on the front door.

"Get out here, Duck and Mike!" he yelled.

When Duck and Mike came outside, Granddeddy looked at Peanut and then at them, said, "Don't you leave my baby no more."

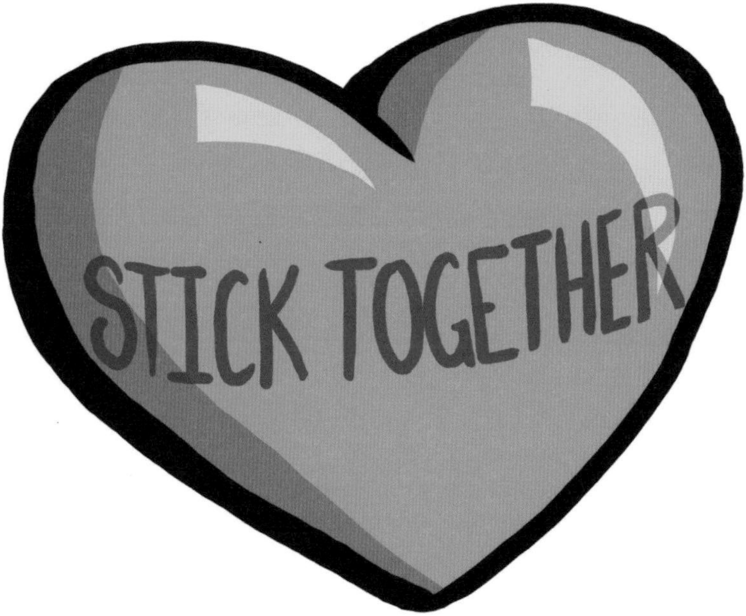
STICK TOGETHER

Granddeddy's Rule
"If Peanut can't go somewhere," he said, "you can't go either."

Peanut and Duck exchanged surprised glances. Granddeddy had a big heart!

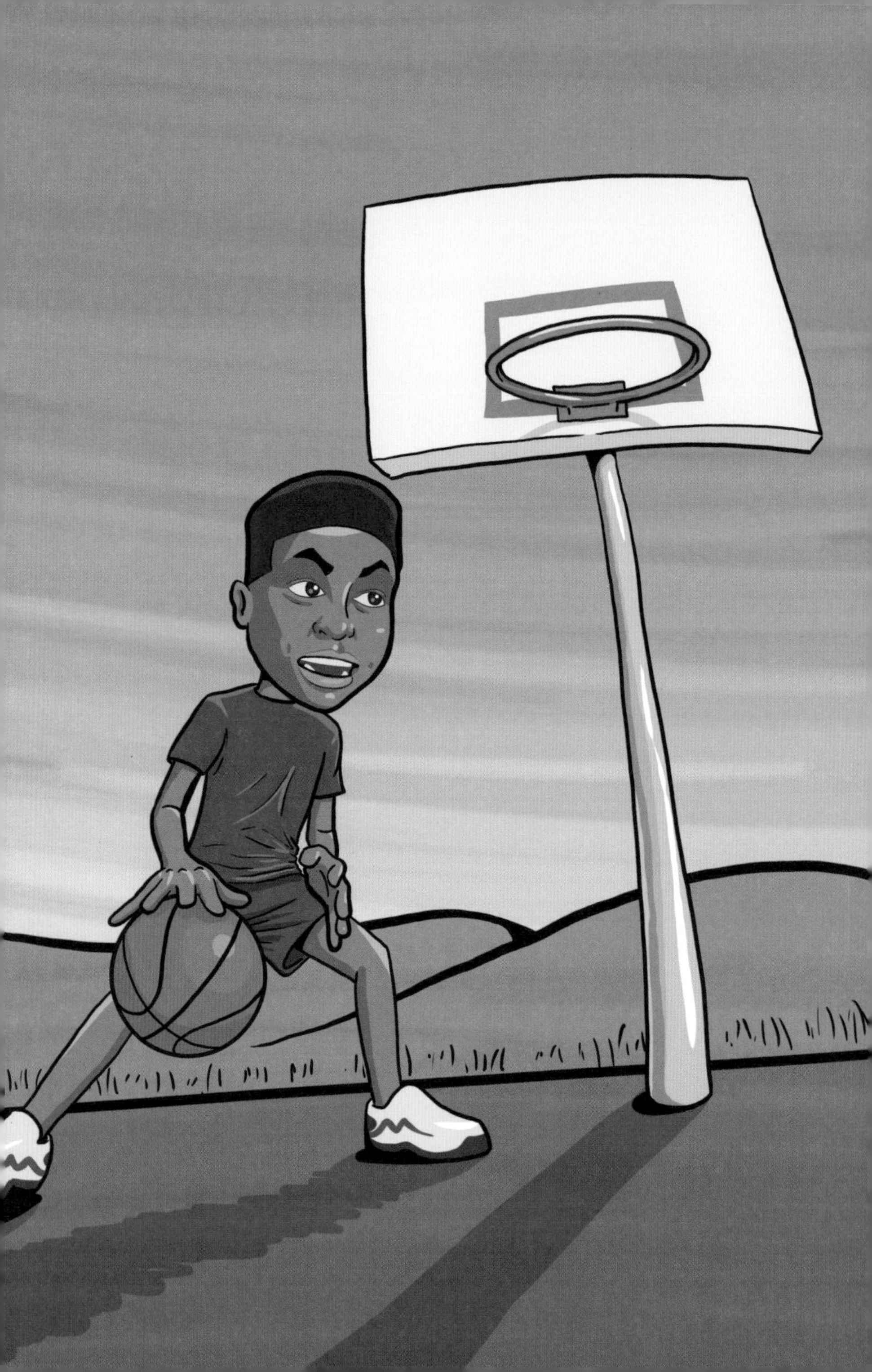

Chapter 5

Game On!

Rule: Regardless of Your Size, Play with Heart

Duck was about two years older than Peanut, but he was *so* much bigger. Their great aunt visited for a few days one summer and highlighted their difference in size.

"Wow, look at how big Duck is!" she said.

Then she turned toward Peanut, who was seven years old at the time: "Ahhh, look at the little one."

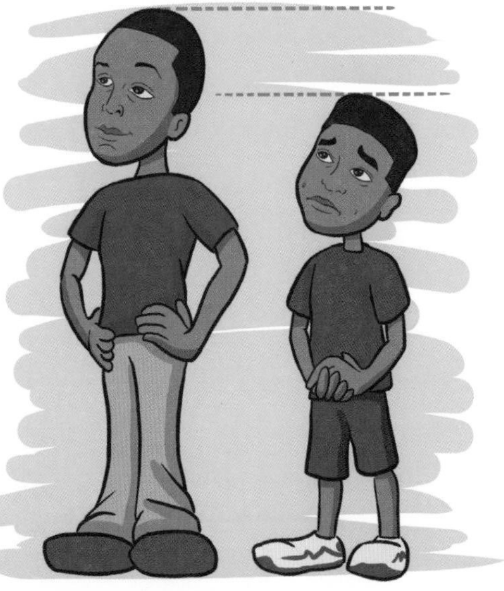

Peanut got angry. "Why do they always call me the little one?" he asked his momma, Tiny.

"Only because you're the youngest," she said. "You're definitely going to grow."

The problem was, Peanut didn't grow fast enough.

When the family went to Six Flags Great America in Gurnee, Illinois, about an hour north of Chicago, Peanut was the *only* cousin who wasn't tall enough for certain rides. He had to watch everyone else have all the fun.

Peanut decided that he couldn't make himself grow any faster, but he could still figure out how to beat Duck in sports. That summer, Peanut started playing one-on-one basketball games against his brother. The winner was the first one to score 11 points. Duck always used his size and strength to earn the win, but Peanut fought him for every point.

"Ugh!" Peanut would yell after he lost another game.

"I'm the big brother," Duck said. "I can't let you win."

Peanut was too feisty to ever give up. His energy and determination to win meant that he got really messy, really fast.

"Don't get grass stains on those pants!" Tiny would yell at the boys as they left the house. Duck would always come home clean; Peanut would usually come home covered in dirt and grass stains.

Duck was a good athlete, but he stayed on his feet. Not Peanut. If they were playing baseball, Peanut would slide into a base, or dive to make a catch. Often, he returned home with a ripped up, sweat-soaked shirt on.

"Not again!" Tiny said.

Peanut would just grin. Getting dirty was half the fun.

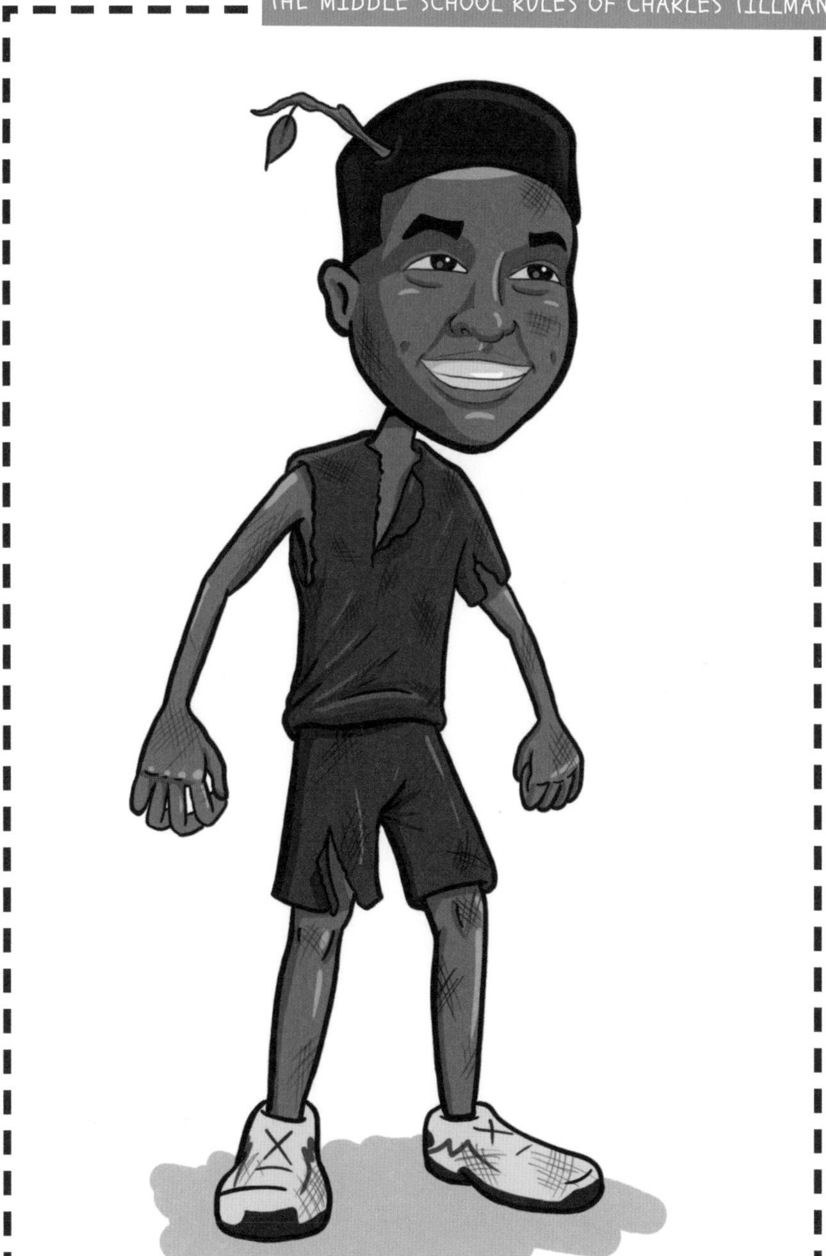

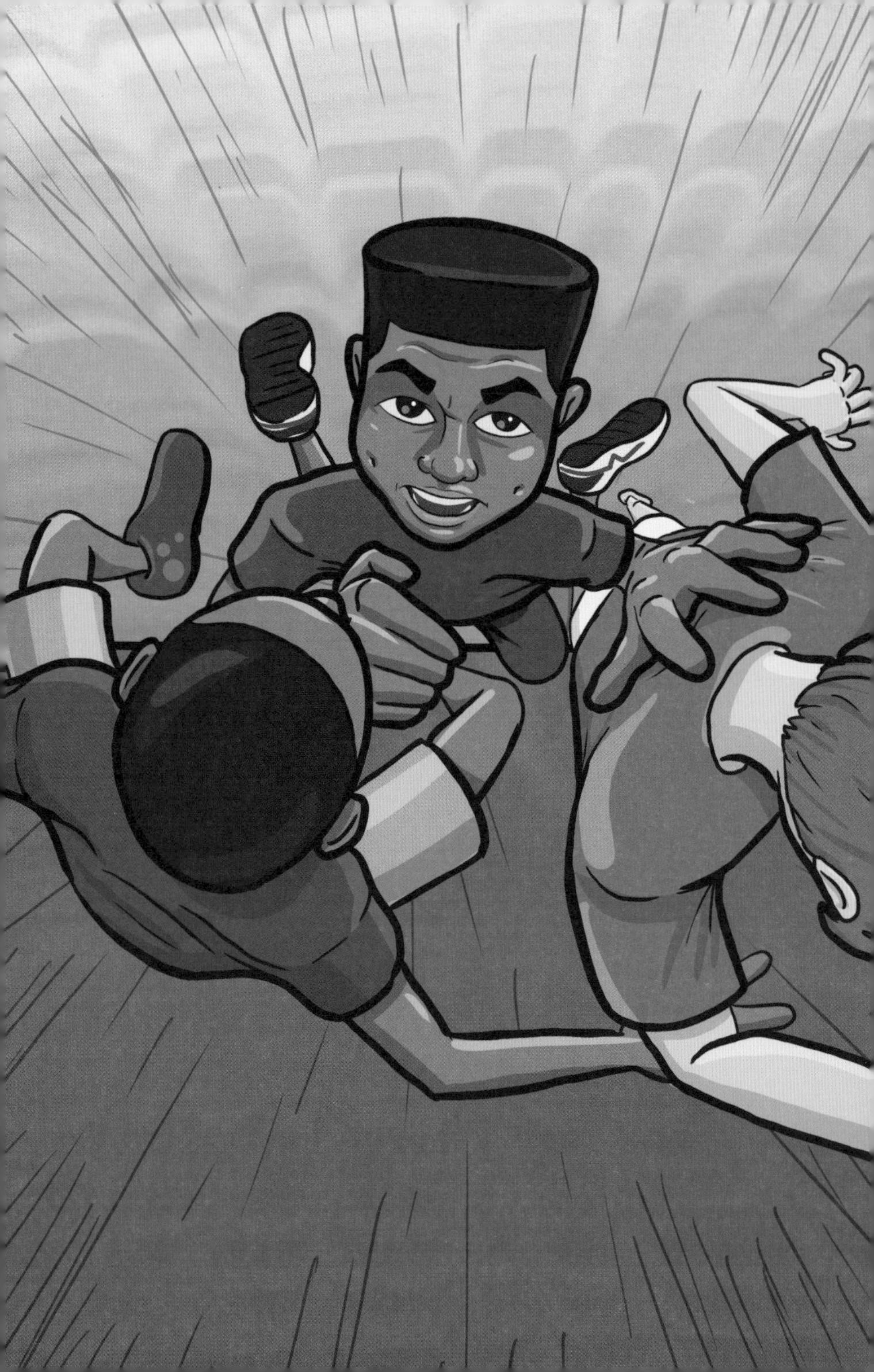

Chapter 6

Duck Protects Peanut

Rule: Stand Up for Your Family

In third grade, Peanut was playing dodge ball. He accidentally drilled a classmate named Brad in the face.

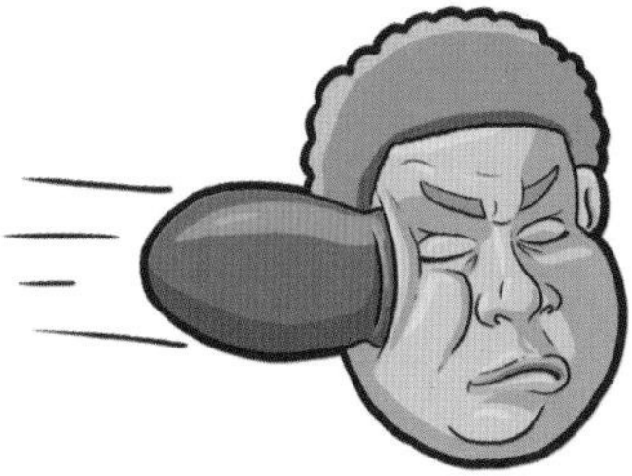

"Ooohhh!" boys and girls simultaneously echoed.

Brad was one of biggest boys in third grade. He was *not* the kid you wanted to mess with, and now he had a big red mark on his right cheek to match his red hair.

Brad got right in Peanut's face: "You're going to pay for that."

Peanut sprinted home after school.

"Duck, Brad wants to beat me up!" Peanut told his brother the whole story. Duck always looked after his little brother. He remembered Grandpa's rule.

When Peanut was done, Duck shrugged and said, "I'll talk to him after school tomorrow."

"After school?" Peanut gasped, "I might not make it until then!"

Duck shook his head. "Anything we do could make Deddy look bad. People look up to him since he's in the Army. We have to handle this carefully."

The next day, Duck passed word to friends that he wanted to meet Brad in a run-down baseball field a block-and-a-half from school. Brad showed up, but he didn't want to fight—not Duck anyway. Kids got nervous around Duck.

Duck was older, of course, but he was also intimidating because he was tall, fast, and didn't say much.

"You got a problem with my brother," Duck softly said, looking Brad straight in his eyes, "then you got a problem with me."

Brad froze. He said nothing.

"Do we have a problem?" Duck asked quietly.

Surrounded by 20 kids, mostly boys, Brad looked down at the ground, kicking up dirt near home plate.

After a few moments, Brad finally spoke: "No, we're good."

Then he turned and walked away.

At dinner that night, Peanut told his parents what Duck did.

Duck didn't know what they would say.

But Deddy smiled, and Momma replied, "Good job looking after your brother. We're proud of you."

Duck soon learned there was one place he didn't need to look out for his brother: on the football field. Peanut could tackle anyone when he was playing football.

Once, while playing with Duck in the backyard, Peanut was an offensive lineman. With a running back behind him, Peanut raced toward Duck and Duck's friend, Warren. The two older boys were playing defense, but Peanut *pancaked* both of them, meaning he knocked them to the ground.

"What in the world?" Warren said, dusting himself off as he got up.

Wow, that was pretty cool! Peanut thought. He was hooked on football.

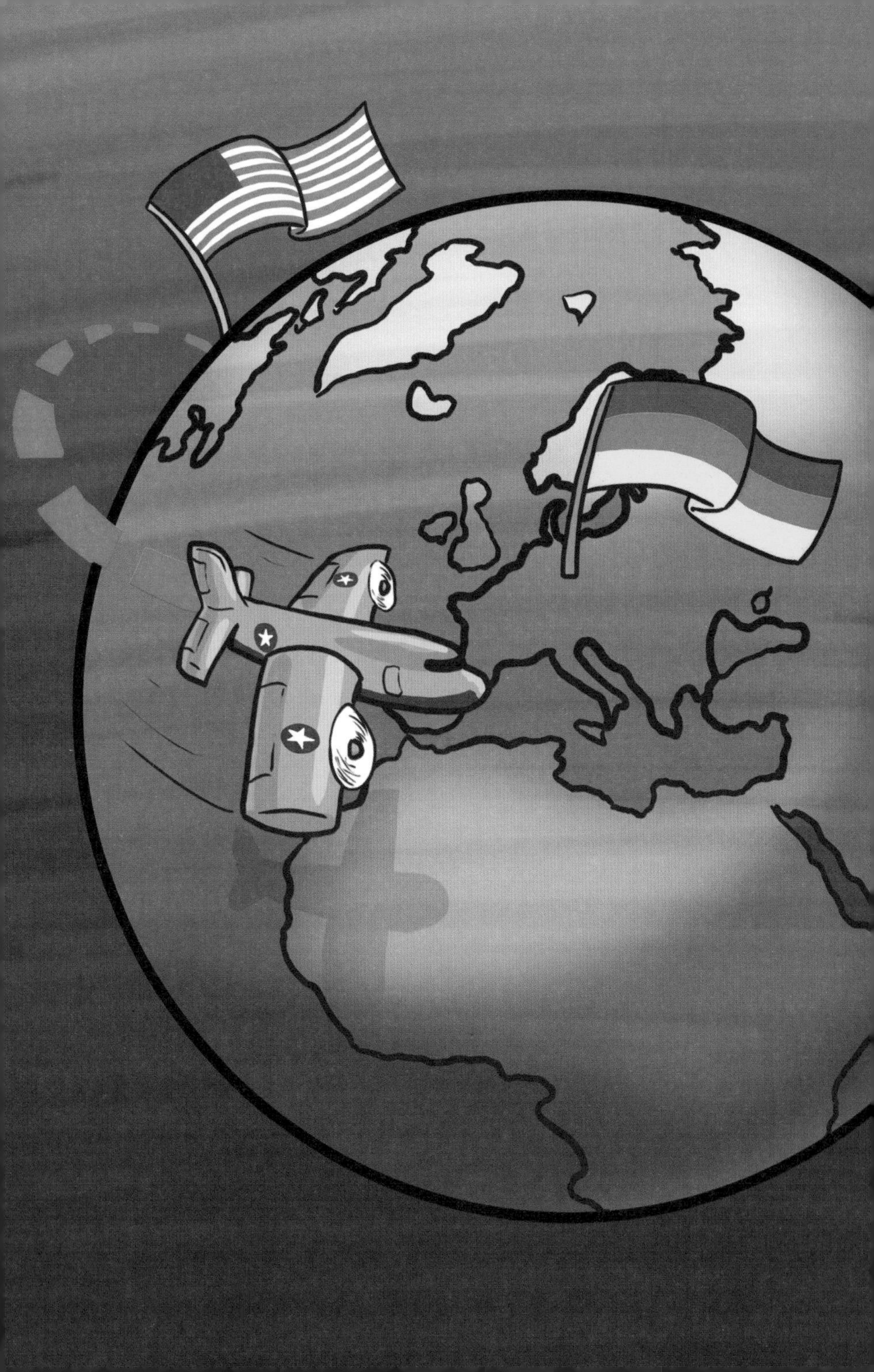

Chapter 7

Seeing the World

Rule: Enjoy Exploration

Peanut dreamed of being an M.P. like Deddy. M.P. stands for *military police*, which meant Lil' Donald was a policeman for the Army. Peanut thought Deddy looked so cool in his green uniform, with *TILLMAN* on a patch over his right chest and *U.S. Army* on a patch over his left chest. Deddy also had a black *M.P.* armband and sometimes wore a green *M.P.* helmet.

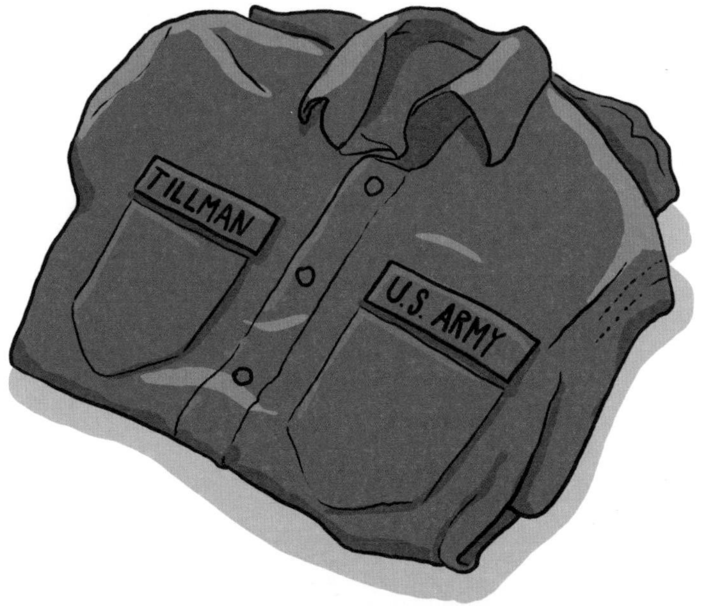
TILLMAN
U.S. ARMY

Peanut thought Deddy looked like G.I. Joe: a popular cartoon and action figure that came with different plastic weapons. G.I. Joe also had some cool army vehicles, but Duck and Peanut got to see the *real* ones.

That's because any chance he could, Lil' Donald would take his sons to see Bradley tanks and Cobra helicopters. And not only would the boys get to see the remarkable military machines, they even got to climb up and sit inside them!

Peanut would imagine himself as different members of the Bradley crew, primarily the driver, commander, and gunner. The driver would control the tank's movement. The commander led the crew, which usually included a couple of scouts, and the gunner would fire the guns—the cannon that shot 200 bullets per minute and the missile launchers that could destroy most tanks over two miles away.

But Peanut only got to be inside a tank and helicopter a few times.

When Lil' Donald switched from M.P. to working in supply, Peanut and Duck got to sit in a "Deuce and a half." That's the nickname for the M35 2½ ton cargo truck. It had six tires and could carry over 10,000 pounds. That means the Deuce and a half could transport most elephants!

Peanut and Duck would sit and pretend they were hauling important weapons and top-secret materials.

There was even a version of the Deuce and a half that could drive underwater. It was nicknamed the "Eager Beaver." The truck could drive underwater because all of the key parts were protected from water. Because the seating area would get flooded, the driver had to wear a snorkel mask, which would let him breathe underwater.

"That is so cool," Peanut told Deddy.

Deddy smiled.

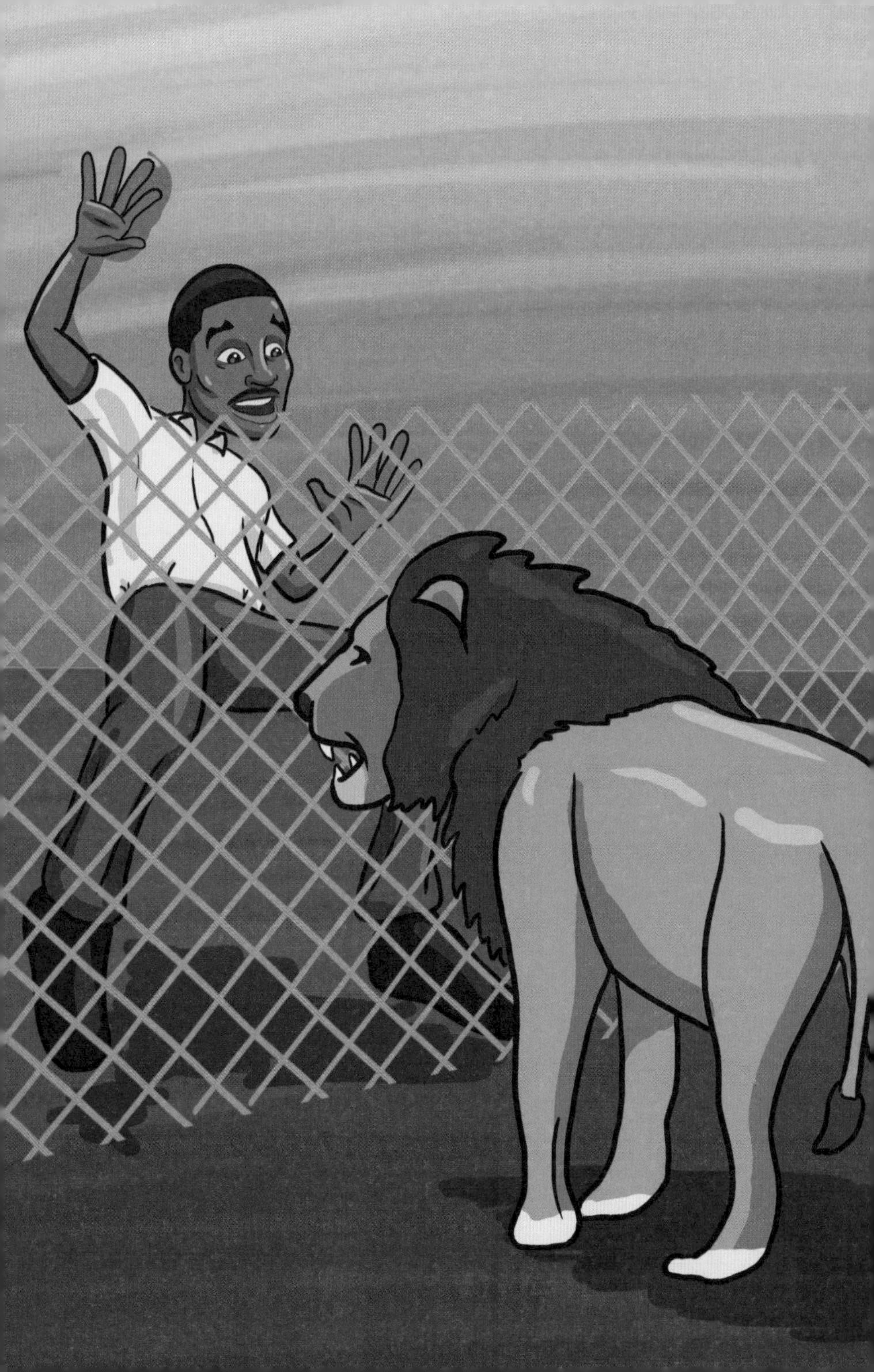

Chapter 8

New Places

Rule: Be Open-minded and Adventurous

Lil' Donald worked a lot. Peanut and his brother didn't mind too much. They knew that when Deddy had time off, he would take the family on an adventure.

The Tillmans loved to explore Germany and other countries in Europe. They liked to visit different parks and restaurants. On the weekends, they would hop in their Mercedes sedan and drive to festivals like Oktoberfest and amusement parks like Phantasialand.

Phantasialand was like Germany's Disney World. Peanut loved it! There were plenty of rides, shows, and snacks. The best snack was the chocolate-covered strawberries. They were made fresh every day.

The spookiest ride was called *Mystery Castle*. It looked like a big stone tower. Riders would get buckled into seats that all faced the middle of the room. Everyone was launched skyward 200 feet then the ride had a pause at the top. A moment later, everyone got dropped. That's like falling 20 floors on an elevator! Peanut wasn't tall enough for that ride, and he was sort of relieved.

NEW PLACES

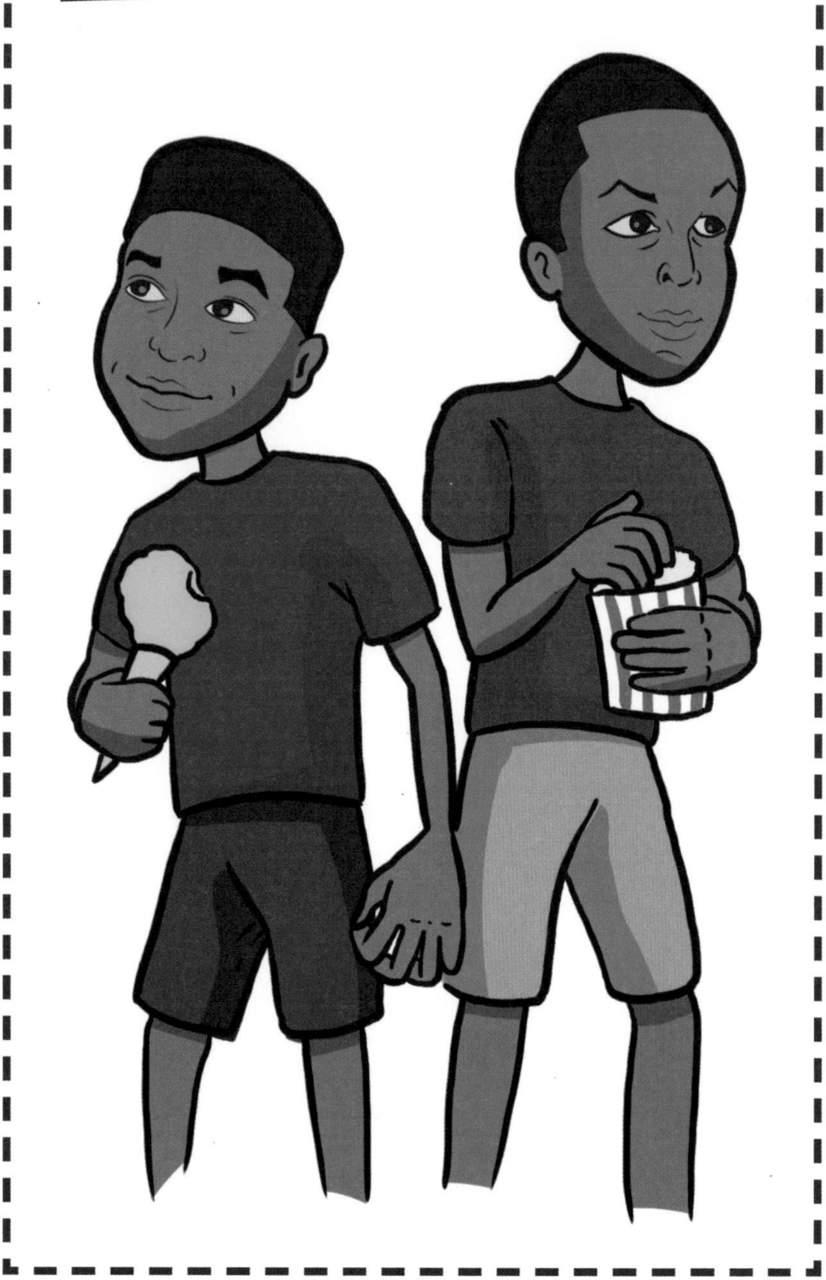

But, of all the adventures as a family, their most memorable one happened at the Frankfurt Zoo. Peanut and Duck saw bears, penguins, orangutans, zebras, and elephants. They ate cotton candy and popcorn. They split a soda.

Then they stopped at the Lion House. Peanut and Duck pressed up against the fence, trying to see the animal nicknamed the "King of Jungle" up close.

"Whoa!" Peanut said. He stood just a couple of feet away from a female lion.

Lil' Donald walked up to the fence too. A male lion appeared to be napping. As Lil' Donald leaned in as close as he could to get a look, the mighty lion roared!

"Ahhhh!!!!" Lil' Donald screamed as he sprinted away from the fence.

Peanut and Duck couldn't stop laughing, and soon everyone around them was laughing too. Lions don't like to be disturbed when they're napping, not even by tough-looking guys in the Army.

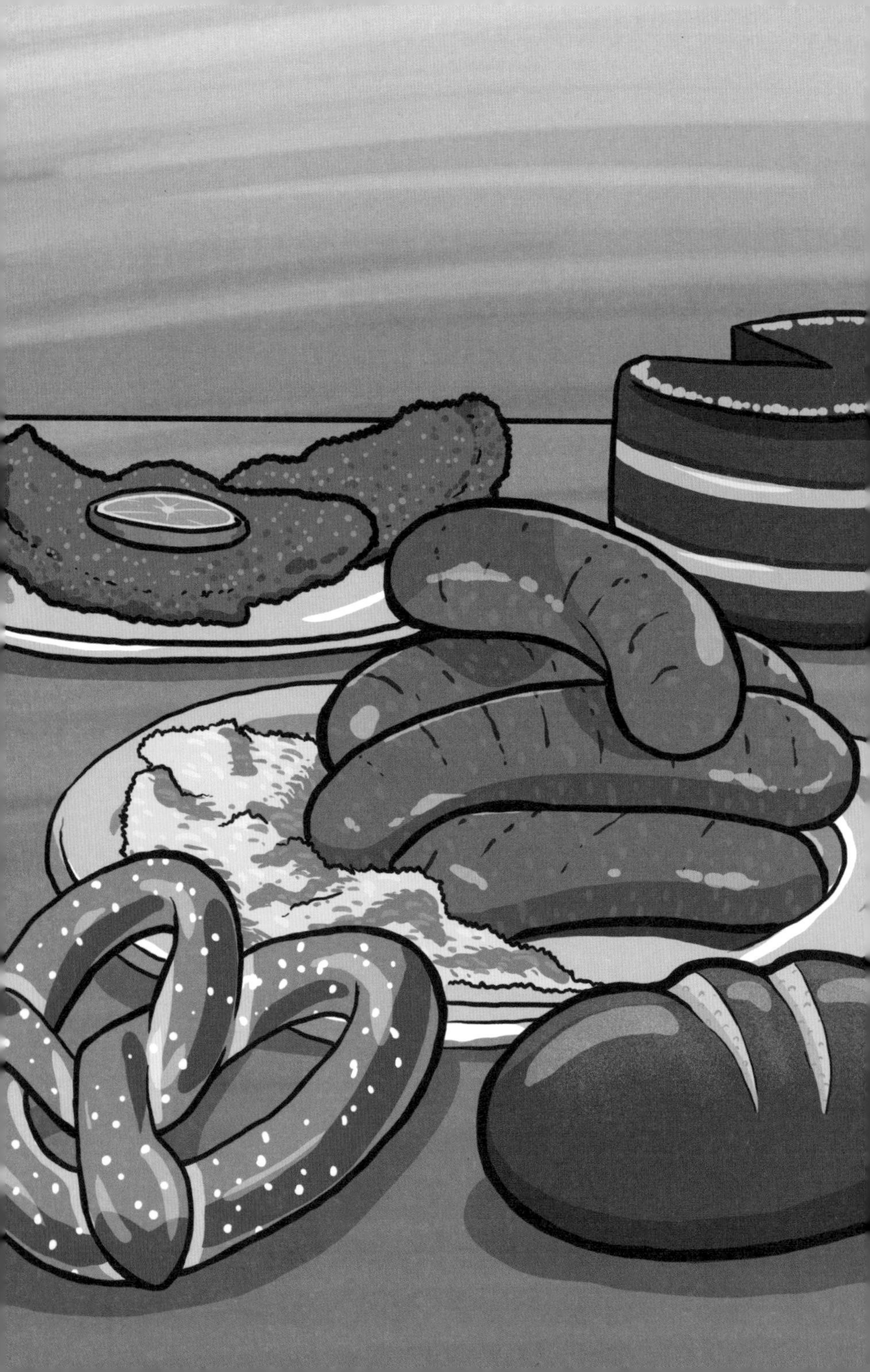

Chapter 9

New Food

In Germany, there's no escaping Oktoberfest. The 16-day festival, originally held to celebrate a royal wedding, is over 200 years old. Today, over six million visitors go to Munich for the world's largest festival!

During Oktoberfest, there were games, bands, and lots of dancing. Plus, there was a lot of food. Peanut was relieved when he saw a hot dog. But Deddy insisted he and Duck eat *real* German food.

"Try this," he said, handing Peanut what looked like a really big chicken nugget.

"What is it? I won't like it," Peanut said, crinkling up his nose. "I *know* I won't like it."

41

NEW FOOD

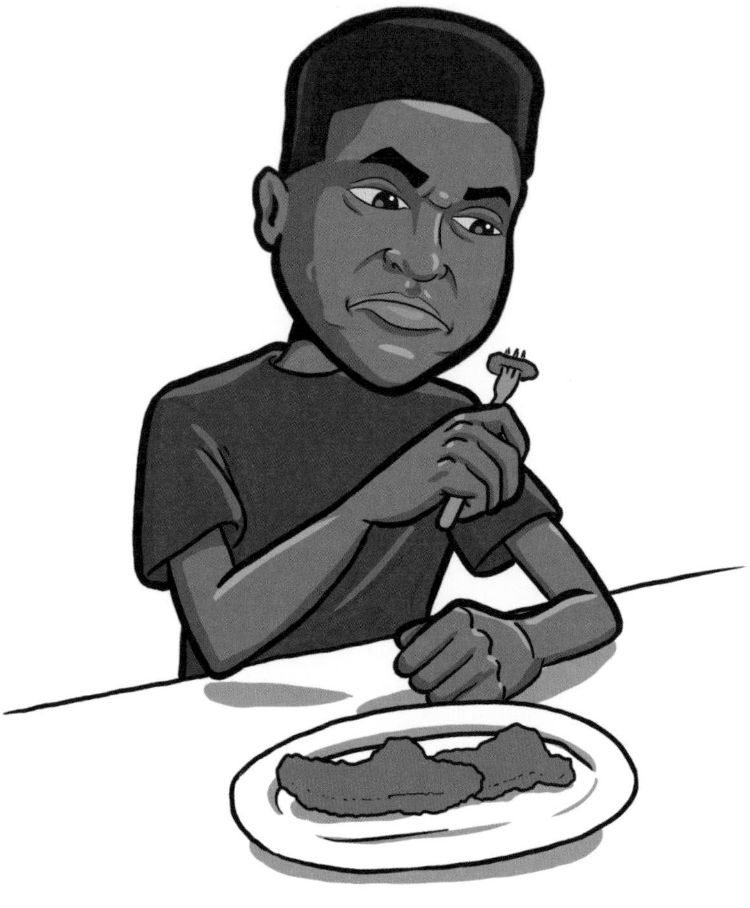

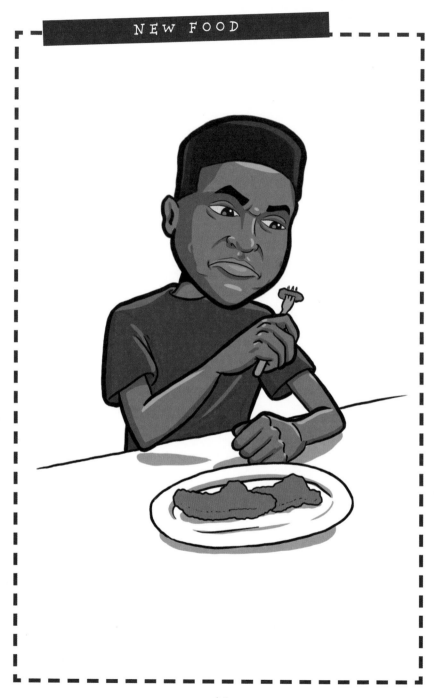

Deddy's Rule

"How do you know if you do or don't like something if you won't try it?" Deddy said.

Reluctantly, Peanut took a bite.

"Mmm, it's really good, Deddy!"

"That's called Weiner Schnitzel," Deddy said. The name made Peanut laugh, but he finished every bite.

Peanut tried a lot more foods: *Brotchen* (a roll), *Bratwurst* (a sausage), and *Currywurst*. Currywurst is a fried pork sausage seasoned with ketchup and curry powder.

Peanut decided that Currywurst was his favorite food to eat—but Weiner Schnitzel still had the funniest name.

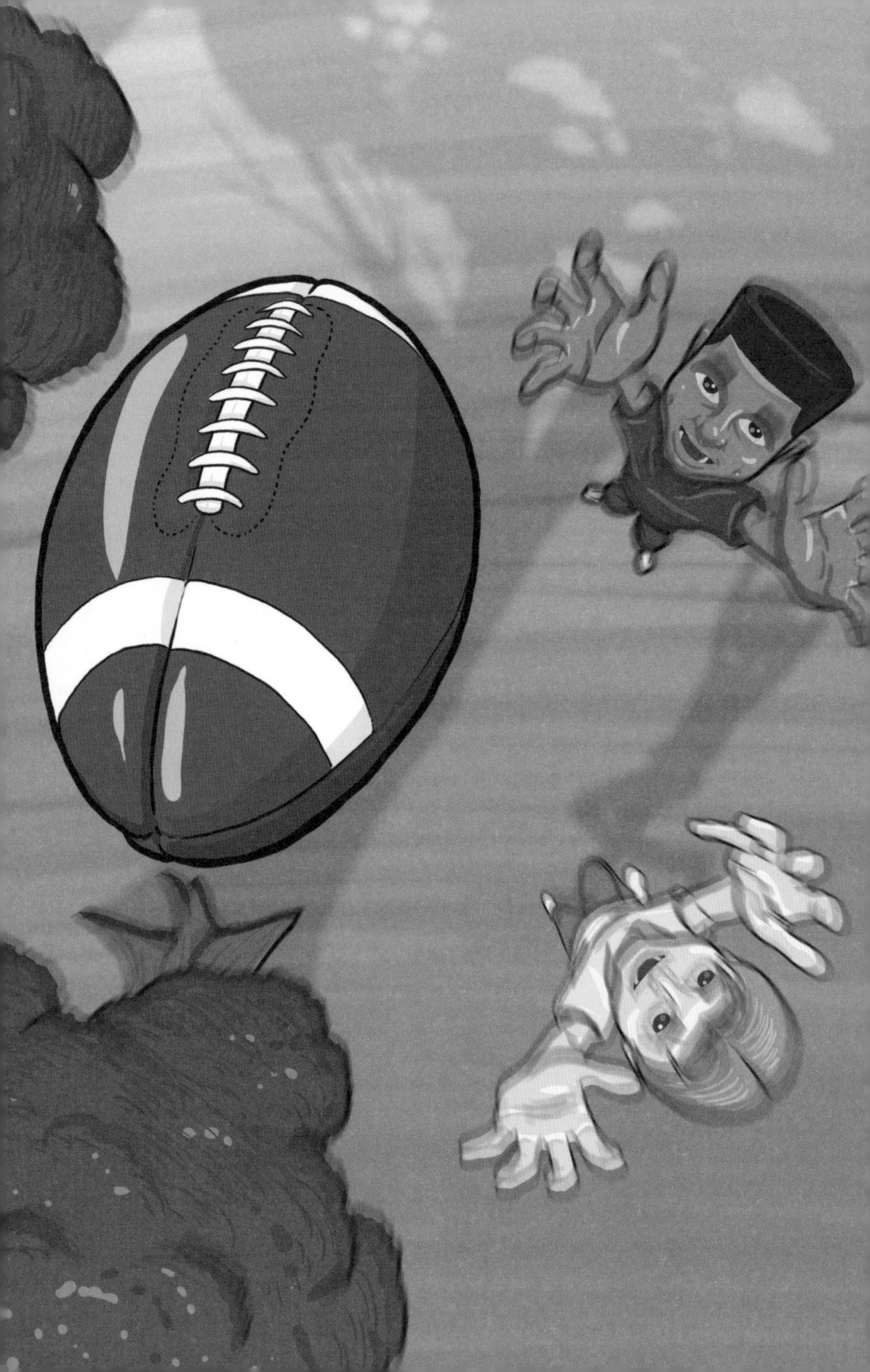

Chapter 10

New Friend

The Tillmans moved to different Army posts in Germany. Some of the posts were very small, and military families had to live in German towns. Peanut was eight years old when his family lived in a town named Einselthum. A lot of American kids were around, and they played together all the time. One of their staple activities was playing football.

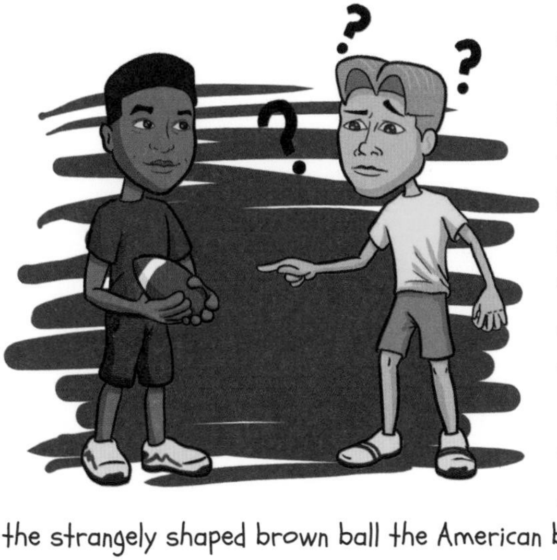

On a bright, sunny Saturday morning, the boys were playing football when a blond, blue-eyed boy walked up. He watched in wonder, clearly confused by the American sport.

The boy was German, and he had never before seen the strangely shaped brown ball the American boys were playing with.

"Uh, what game do you play?" the German boy said slowly, in broken English.

Peanut was puzzled.

"This is football," Peanut said.

Now the German boy really looked puzzled.

"No, football has round ball," the German boy said.

Everyone was confused.

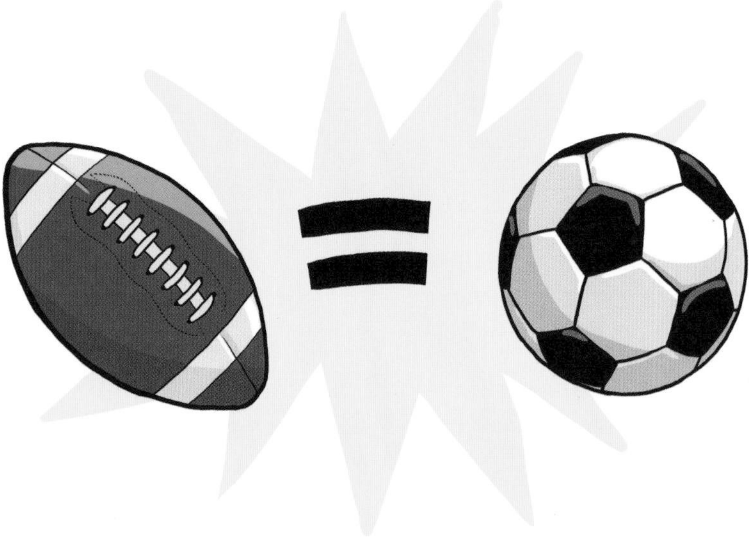

Then Duck realized what the problem was. "He's talking about soccer!"

In the United States, the sport with a round ball that players kick is called *soccer*. Everywhere else, it's called *football*.

Peanut learned the German boy's name was Kai. They were very different. Peanut thought about something his momma always told him.

Momma's Rule

"Be lovable; be nice," Momma said. "Kindness will take you a long way and make you a lot of friends."

Peanut and Kai became friends even though Kai didn't speak much English, and Peanut didn't speak much German. They learned new words every day, and they managed to communicate with body language.

Peanut taught Kai about American football. Kai taught Peanut how to skateboard and play soccer.

Their favorite game to play together was one Peanut helped make up. They'd throw a ball up in the air, and everyone scrambled to retrieve it. Whoever got the ball would try to run to a tree. That would count as a score. But if you were tackled, you would have to throw the ball up again.

Peanut couldn't speak German very well, but he had learned an important lesson: kids all over the world love sports.

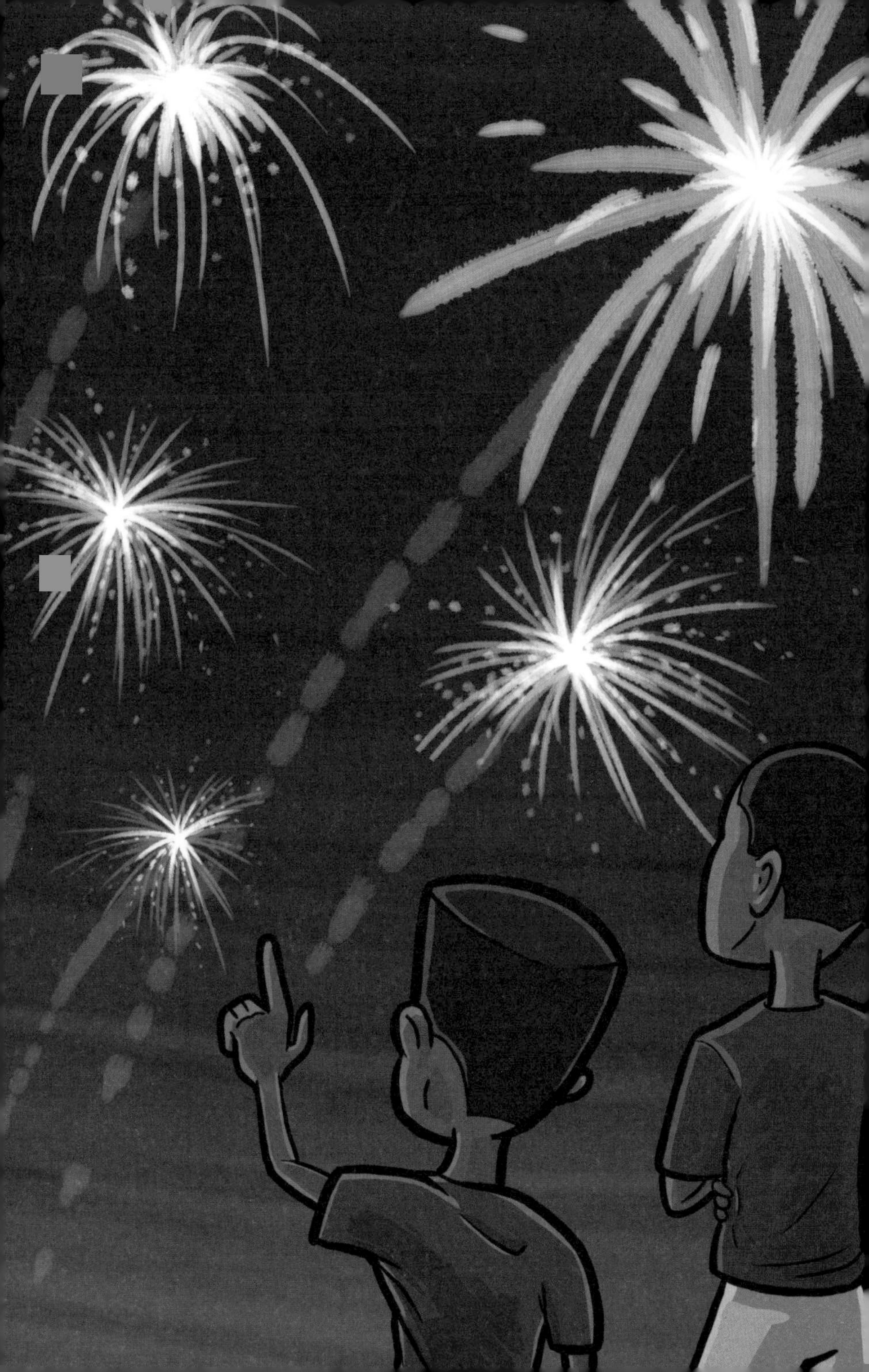

Chapter 11

Fireworks in Germany

Peanut and his family loved discovering and exploring Europe.

But everyone in the family missed one thing from home: American television.

While they were in Germany, the Tillmans could only get one English-language television station: the Armed Forces Network. AFN aired programs from major American-based, English-language networks such as ABC, CNN, NBC, and ESPN. All the other TV channels were in German.

Meine Güte! That's German for, "Good grief!"

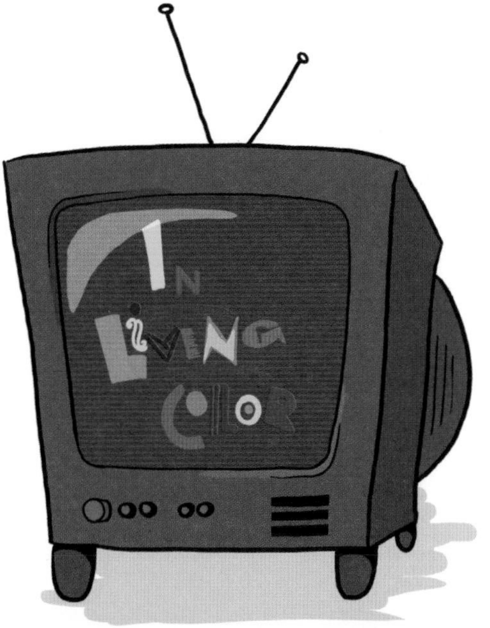
IN LIVING COLOR

Peanut's extended family back in Chicago recorded television programs on videotapes then shipped them in boxes to Germany every couple of months.

"Don't skip the commercials," Peanut would remind his relatives.

When the Tillmans got a box of videotapes, they'd eat dinner in front of the TV and watch the shows for hours. Tiny liked soap operas and the Soul Train Music Awards, but Peanut, Lil' Donald, and Duck liked football and basketball games.

The whole family enjoyed *In Living Color* and *The Cosby Show*: two important programs starring brown-skinned actors and actresses. Those were the two shows the family watched most.

Something else Peanut and his family missed from the United States was the 4th of July celebration each year. On July 4, 1776, the U.S. celebrated its *independence* from Great Britain.

When they lived in Chicago, Peanut and Duck would watch the July 4th fireworks off of Navy Pier, right on Lake Michigan. Although they were miles and miles away, the boys could see the bright colors light up the dark sky.

"Whoa!" Peanut and Duck would scream.

The show seemed to last forever, a sequence of fireworks that exploded, one after another. *Whoosh... Boom! Whoosh... Boom!*

Peanut's favorite firework would sail into the air, burst, and shoot light outward, burning out and leaving a trail that looked like the legs of spiders. Then there would be a dramatic pause for what seemed like hours, not minutes. It was time for the Grand Finale.

For five minutes or more, fireworks would pop, pop, pop, making the pitch black of night display the kaleidoscope of colors seen at dusk.

One 4th of July, when Peanut was 11, he and Duck were playing basketball with a big group of American boys. They were on Husterhoeh Kaserne, an Army post near Pirmasens, Germany, about 15 miles from the border of France.

Many families gathered at the park for a barbeque. They grilled hot dogs, hamburgers, and bratwurst, and there was potato salad, cookies, and strudel.

After they ate, the boys played more basketball until it started to get dark. Then one of the older boys, Jesse, walked over to his backpack.

"Come check *this* out," Jesse said.

All the boys gathered around the backpack, trying to peek at

Chapter 19

Football Dream

Rule: Dare to Dream

Peanut loved hanging out with his cousins Camillá, Denise, Dwan, and Lil' Greg. But he was closest to Camillá. She was only three months older. Peanut and Camillá just "clicked" and always enjoyed playing and talking together.

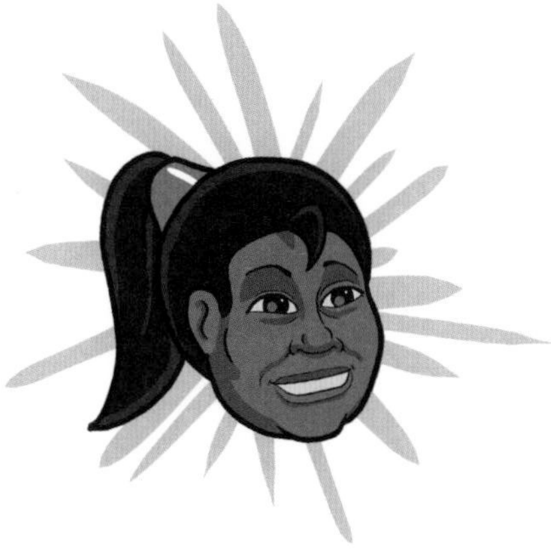

"We're twins," Peanut and Camillá jokingly told relatives.

Peanut appreciated that Camillá was always willing to toss the football around with him and talk about sports.

"Peanut, I know you want to be a football player when you grow up," Camillá said one day. "You know what that means, right?"

Peanut had no clue what Camillá was talking about.

"That means people are going to want your autograph!" she said.

An autograph is a signature from a famous person. It's

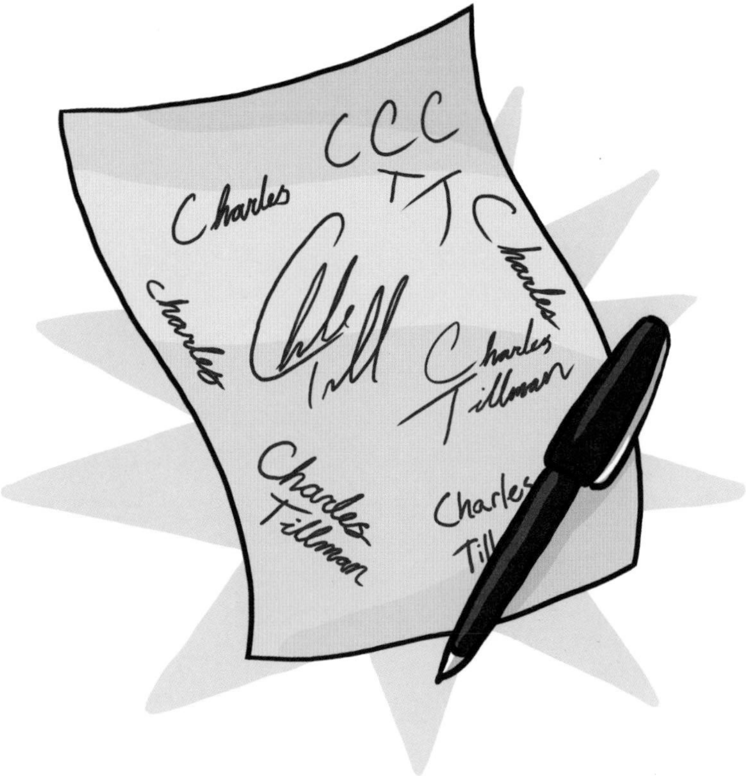
CCC
Charles
Charles
Charles
Charles Tillman
Charles Tillman
Charles
Till

a quick way to provide something special to fans. When a fan sees someone they admire, they may only have a few seconds to capture the moment. An autograph is a way for the fan to remember the moment forever.

Peanut and Camillá hustled inside. Camillá grabbed a pen and four blank sheets of paper.

"Now sign your name," Camillá told Peanut.

Peanut slowly and clearly signed his name, *Charles Tillman*, with all the letters the same height.

"No, no!" Camillá said. "You're signing too slowly. If you're going to be a famous football player, you're going to have to sign a lot of things."

Peanut tried again, only faster.

"How's this?" he asked.

"Much better," Camillá said. "But the key is the C."

Later that night at home, Peanut sat at the dining room table. He concentrated very hard.

"What are you doing?" Momma asked him.

"Practicing how I'm going to sign my name when I'm in the NFL," Peanut said, not even looking up.

Tiny knew Peanut loved football. He talked about the sport often, and Chicago Bears running back Walter Payton was his hero. She knew the chances of Peanut making it to the NFL were not great.

Each season, more than 1.1 million high school athletes play football, and less than 0.2 percent make it to the NFL. That's only 2,200 players!

Tiny didn't want to crush her son's dream.

"Well," Momma said, "your signature sure looks nice."

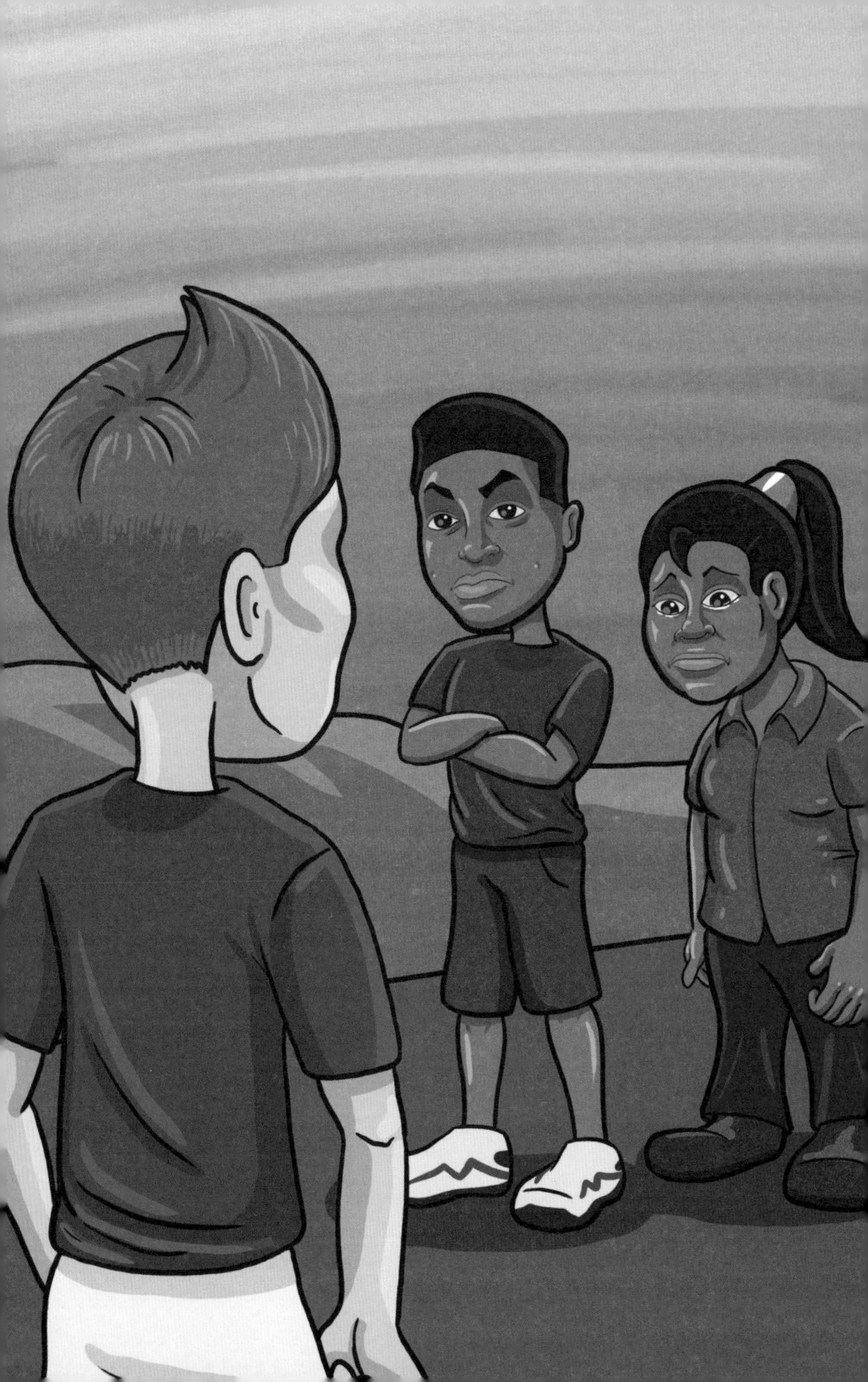

Chapter 20

Encourage; Don't Discourage

Peanut saw his cousins a lot the summer after he finished sixth grade.

He and Duck would get dropped off at Grandma Alice's house. The cousins would watch TV shows and movies, go to the mall, or play sports and games with other kids in Grandma Alice's neighborhood.

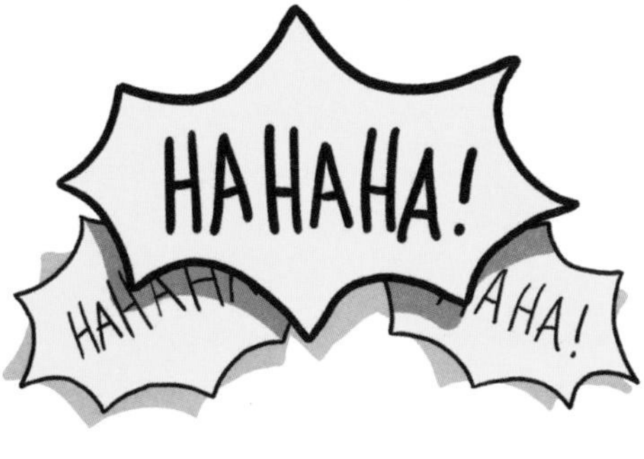
HAHAHA!
AHA!

Nick regularly joined them. He lived three houses away, and he liked to laugh. He cracked jokes all the time, making fun of what people said and did.

"Duck, why do you walk so slow?" Nick said, impersonating the deliberate way Peanut's brother moved.

One afternoon, after a spirited neighborhood game of football, Nick targeted Camillá.

"I noticed something," Nick said with a grin. "How come all of you cousins are super skinny except for Camillá? Are you sure you're part of the family?"

ENCOURAGE; DON'T DISCOURAGE

Several of the neighborhood boys started to laugh.

"Hey Duck and Peanut," Nick said, "are you guys so skinny because Camillá eats all the food?"

More laughs.

Peanut was upset. He knew Camillá was sensitive about her weight. She had confided to Peanut—who she trusted—that she often felt like the "chunky" cousin.

"There's nothing wrong with you," Peanut would tell Camillá. "You are perfect just the way you are." He would encourage Camillá to go for walks and exercise, but he never shamed her.

That's what Nick was doing, and Peanut wouldn't allow it.

He didn't like to confront people, but he thought about one of his momma's rules.

Momma's Rule

"Treat people like you want to be treated," Momma said. "And if you see someone being bullied or mistreated, then you should step in and stop it."

Momma demanded that Peanut and Duck be kind and loving to others; she didn't like talk that cut people down and hurt their feelings.

Peanut noticed Camillá start to lower her head. Her lip quivered. She looked like she was about to cry.

"That's not funny," Peanut said firmly to Nick. "Stop talking about my cousin!"

Peanut looked Nick right in the eyes and didn't blink. He was very, very serious.

Nick got the message.

"Sheesh," he said, "I was just joking around. You guys are no fun. I'm going home."

A few hours later, when they had a moment alone, Camillá hugged Peanut.

"Thanks for having my back, twin," she said.

Peanut didn't think it was a big deal. He was just doing what was right—watching out for Camillá.

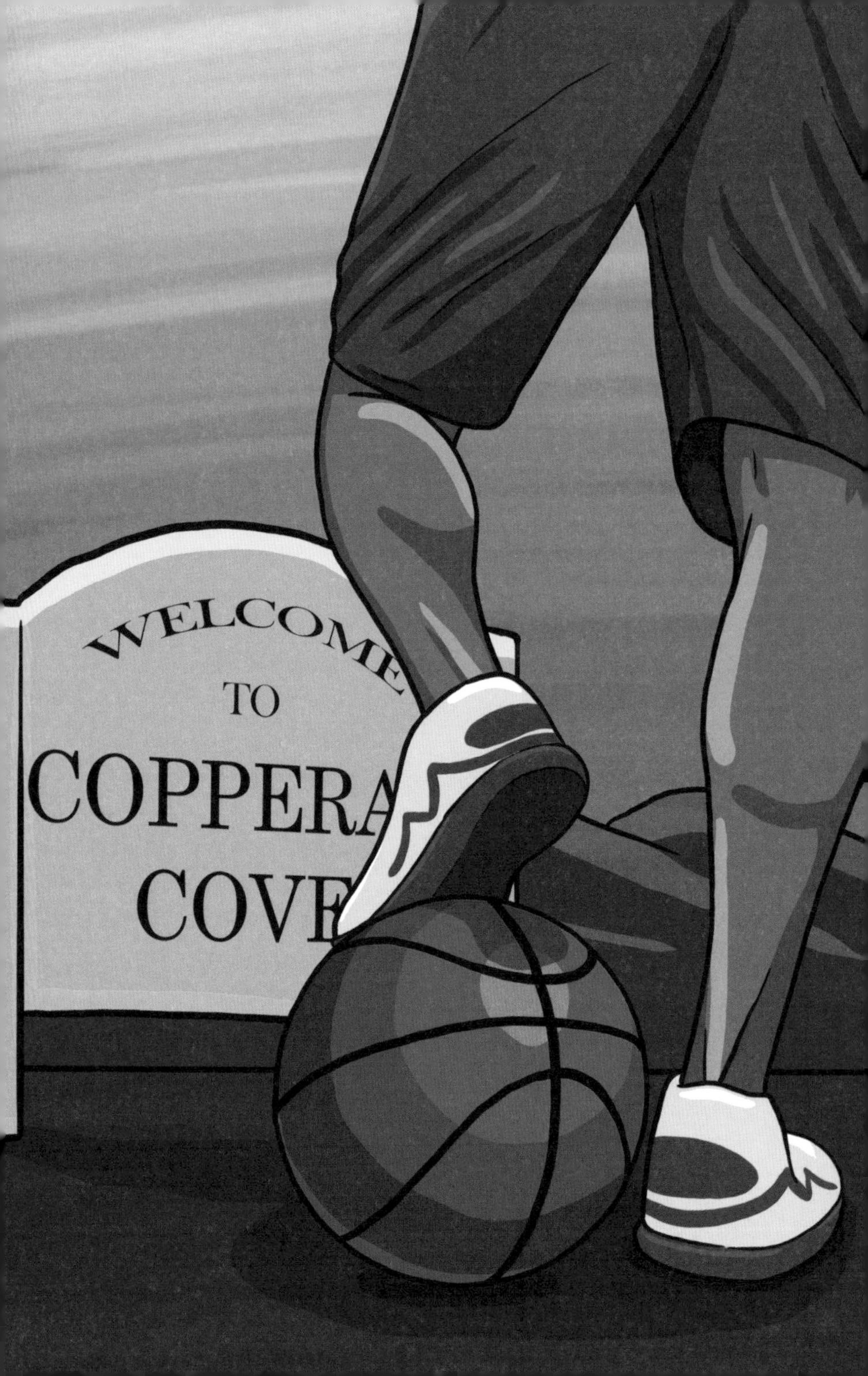
WELCOME
TO
COPPERA
COVE

Chapter 21

Cove

Rule: Make a Good First Impression

After a few months in Sherman, Peanut and his family moved to Copperas Cove, which was three-and-a-half hours south. Locals called it "Cove," and its nickname was City of Five Hills.

Copperas Cove started as a small farming and cattle ranching community in the late 1800s. But Cove grew much bigger when the Army built Fort Hood in the 1940s.

Peanut's family moved into a house on Main Street. There were trees on the right side and in the backyard. Peanut and Duck were very excited because there were lots of boys in their neighborhood and several playgrounds with basketball hoops.

On their first Saturday in Copperas Cove, Peanut headed to the nearest basketball court. Because he moved around so much, Peanut wasn't shy about introducing himself to others.

"Hey, how you doing?" Peanut said to a boy lacing up his shoes. "My name is Charles but everyone calls me *Peanut*."

"Nice to meet you, Peanut," the boy said. "My name is Kevin. And that's *Rico*."

Peanut learned that football

season had just ended at Copperas Cove Junior High School. But after his first day of school, Peanut played basketball with some of his new friends. Peanut was fast, and he was ferocious.

"Who is that?" Coach Ranes asked.

After the boys played a few pickup games, Coach Ranes approached Peanut.

"I'm Coach Ranes: I'm the P.E. teacher and basketball coach," he said. "Where did you come from?"

"Oh, I just moved here," Peanut said.

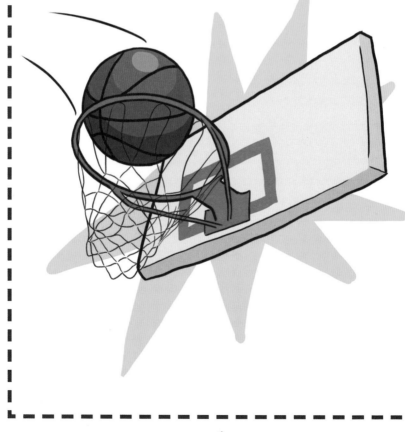

The basketball team had tryouts the week before, and coaches had already picked their A and B teams. The A team had the better players. Coach Ranes decided to give Peanut a special tryout because he was new to the school. Peanut had to run, jump, shoot, pass, and defend for 20 minutes.

Coach Ranes liked what he saw.

"You're going to be on the A team," he told Peanut afterwards.

Peanut would be playing with Kevin and Rico! Kevin was skinny, but he was the team's best outside shooter. Rico was a good dribbler and scorer. Peanut's specialty was defense.

Coach Ranes always had Peanut guard the other team's best player.

The A team dominated opponents.

Jack Welch, the head football coach of Copperas Cove High School, liked to check in on the young athletes in his community and he stopped in to watch a few games.

Peanut stood out. He wasn't the best basketball player on his team, but he had quick hands, which helped him steal the ball a lot. And he could jump high and run fast.

"I hope he plays football, too," Coach Welch said to an assistant coach. "That kid is a *hoss*."

In Texas, being called a hoss is a compliment. It means you're an impressive person.

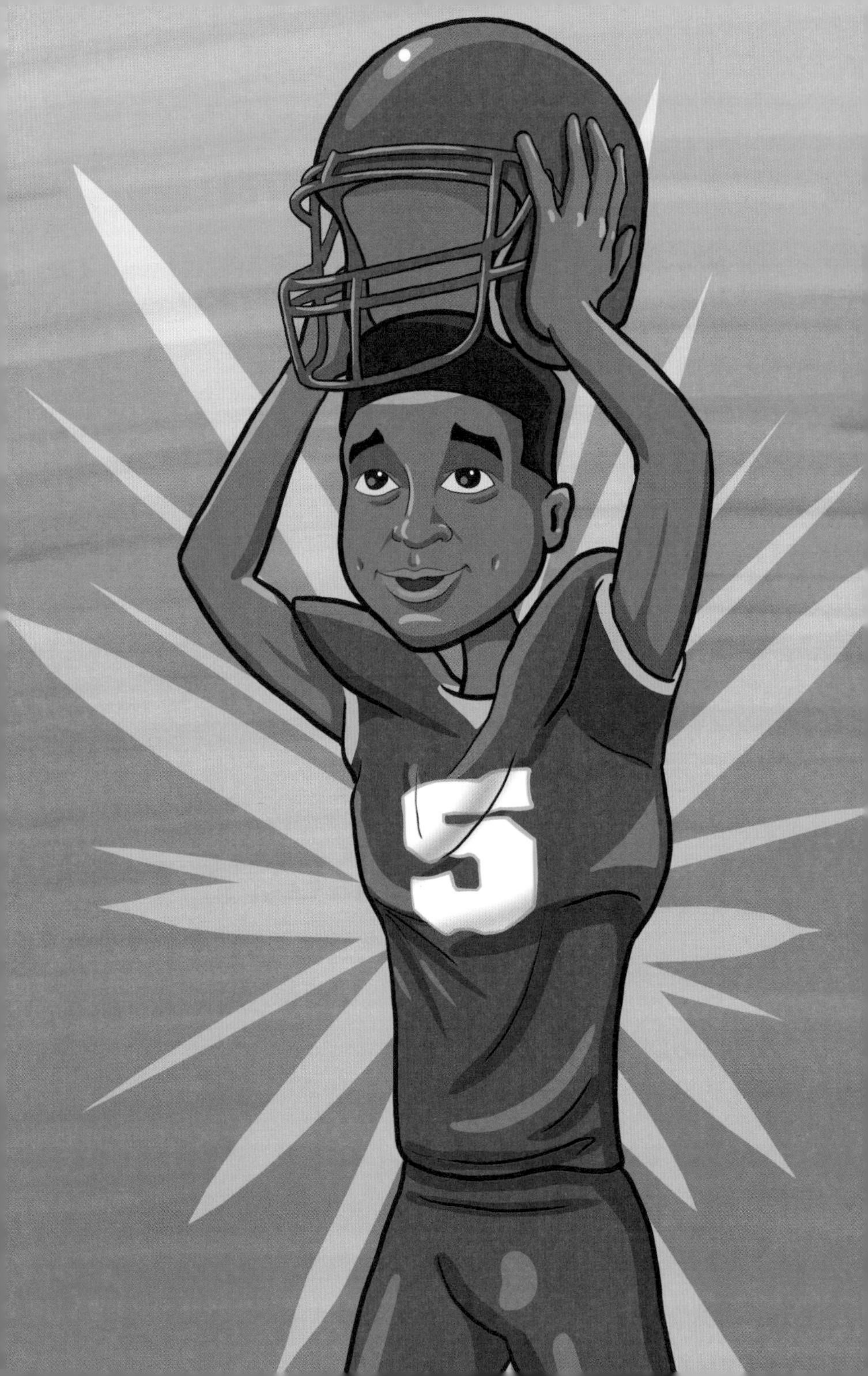
5

Chapter 22 Finally, Football

Peanut walked into the boys' locker room at Copperas Cove Junior High School. He was an 8th grader now, and he was on a football team for the first time! His family's rules had guided him through many moves and different schools. But in eighth grade, it was time for Peanut to learn some new rules.

Earlier in the year, Coach Welch had arrived to lead the struggling football program. He had coached at several colleges before taking over the Copperas Cove High School Bulldawgs. The Bulldawgs played in the largest conference in Texas but had never had much success in football—the state's most popular sport. The season before Coach Welch arrived, the Bulldawgs had a 1–9 record.

One of Coach Welch's first moves was to merge the middle and high school programs. He would create a pipeline so assistant coaches and players could grow together. Also, the middle schoolers would run the same spread offense and play the same attacking defense as the varsity players.

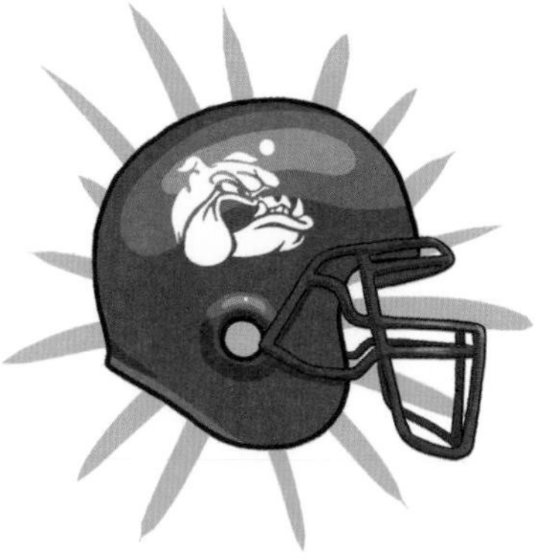

Peanut was assigned to play safety on defense and receiver on offense.

Coach Roberts was his receivers' coach, and he repeated one rule every day at practice.

Coach Roberts' Rule

"You have to have liquid hands, soft hands," he said. "Catch the ball gently."

Coach also had a favorite drill. Peanut would go up to the blue padding on the yellow field goal post. He would extend his arms out, with his chest right up against the blue padding. Then Coach Roberts would throw a pass toward his hands.

This drill emphasized catching the ball only with your hands and not using your body to help control it. Coach Roberts would throw five balls, and then the next receiver would wrap his arms around the goal post and try to catch the ball.

Peanut did that for 15 minutes every day.

Before his first game, Peanut walked into the middle school locker room. He was assigned the No. 5 jersey. Hanging in his stall was a bright blue helmet, bearing a cartoonish bulldog with sharp teeth, as well as a blue jersey with white numbers and a yellow outline.

"Wow..."

Teammates started to trickle into the locker room. The game wasn't for 90 minutes, but Peanut was eager to put on his jersey. He slipped his head through the shoulder pads and plopped the helmet onto his head. He felt like a real football player.

In the game, Peanut also caught his first touchdown off a reverse pass. On the play, the quarterback tossed the ball to the running back, who sprinted to his left. The running back then flipped the ball to a receiver who started on the left side of the field but headed into the backfield. Peanut, who was the receiver lined up on the right side, was wide open because the defenders followed the ball away from him.

When the other receiver got toward the middle of the field, he launched the ball toward the right sideline, where Peanut was all alone. Peanut made the catch and ran 25 yards into the end zone for a touchdown.

The Bulldawgs won their first game 17–6!

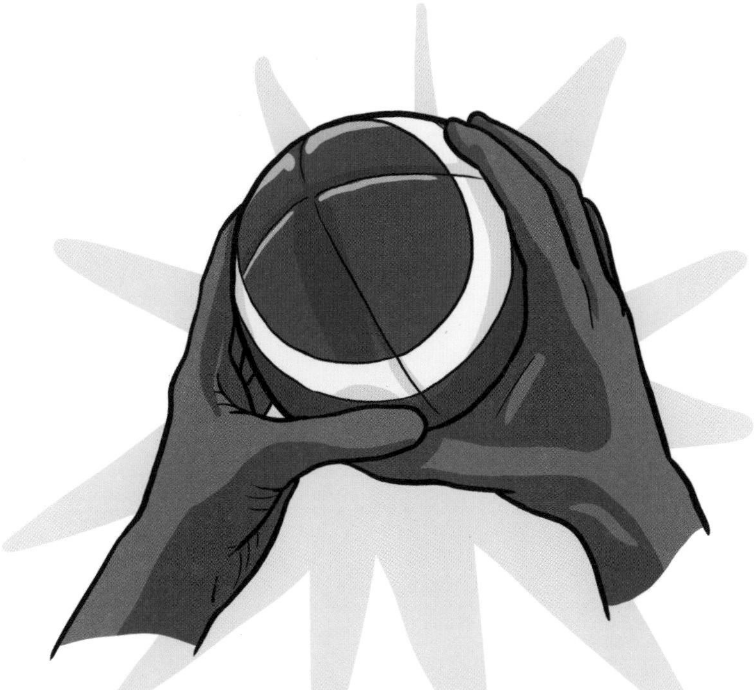

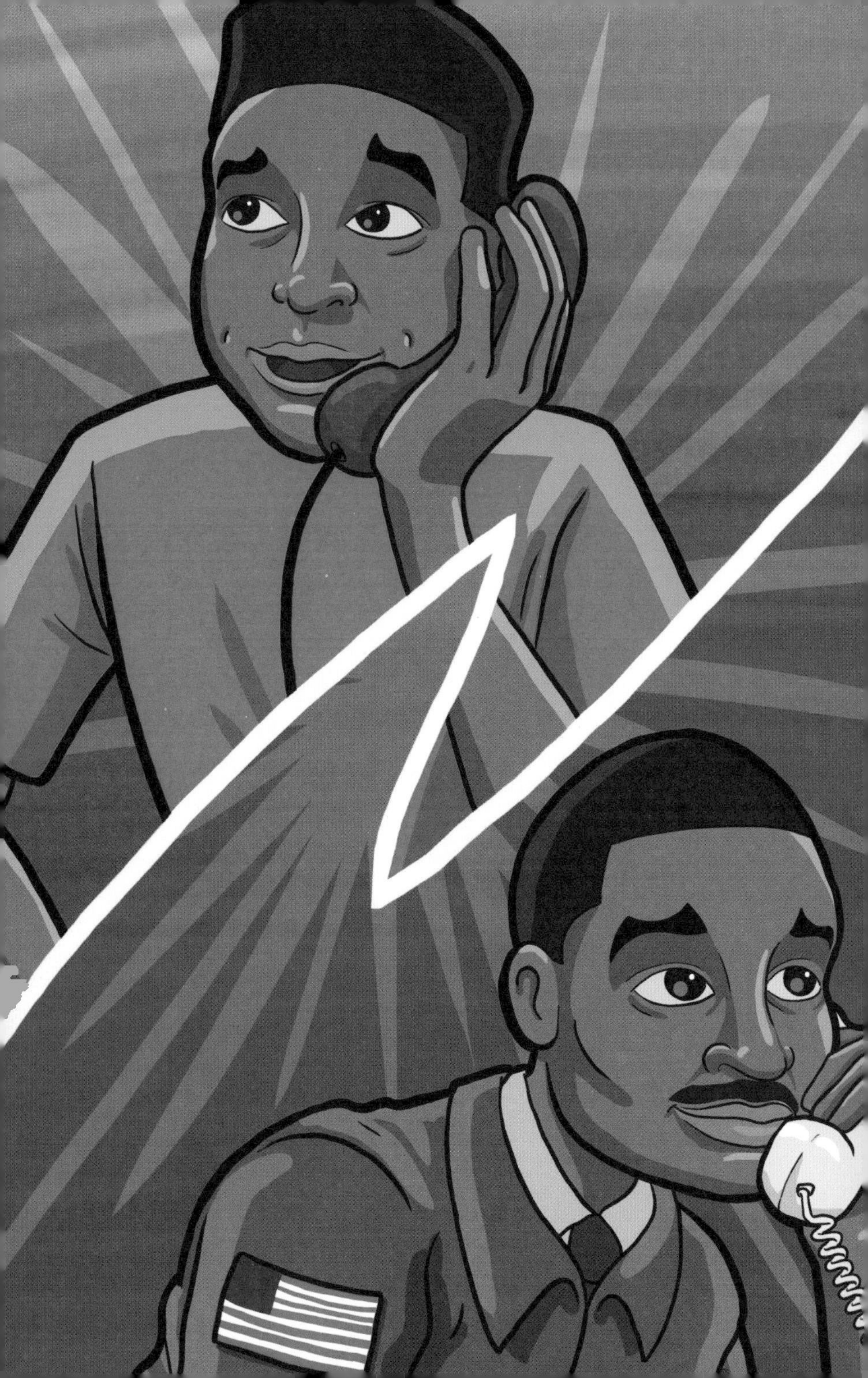

Chapter 23

TDY

Rule: Military Responsibilities Can Be Tough for a Family

Peanut's momma and brother watched his first touchdown in his first game.

"What a great touchdown, Peanut!" Momma said. "We're so proud of you!"

But Deddy wasn't there. He was on a Temporary Duty assignment. Temporary Duty is also called TDY, and it means an Army employee is shipped to another post for a short time. Lil' Donald would be in Cuba, an island country south of Florida, for three or four months.

There were some advantages when Deddy went away on TDY. Momma sometimes let the boys sleep in the big bed. She wasn't as strict with her boys because she knew they missed Deddy. She bought them more clothes and shoes. She also went to all their activities, including Peanut's football games.

But it just wasn't the same.

"I wish Deddy were here," Peanut told Duck after a tough loss.

Deddy knew how much Peanut loved football. They talked a lot about it and watched college and pro games together. Peanut wasn't upset with Deddy. He was mature enough to understand that Deddy had a duty to the Army. Besides, in Cuba, Lil' Donald was sad to miss Peanut's games too.

Even worse, Peanut couldn't talk to Deddy very much. At the time, the only way to communicate was by telephone, and international calls—calls from one country to another—were very, very expensive. Lil' Donald could only talk to his family for about 10 minutes once a week.

Peanut noticed that Deddy spent almost all 10 minutes speaking to him and Duck, not Momma. *What's that all about?* Peanut wondered.

Peanut's 8th grade football team wasn't very good, and they finished the season 4-4.

Basketball started a few weeks after football ended. Midway through one practice, Peanut's teammates stopped their drill and looked toward the gym entrance.

Lil' Donald, in full uniform, jogged toward the court.

"Deddy is home!" Peanut screamed, running toward him. He hugged Deddy hard, not wanting to let go. Peanut had missed Deddy a lot.

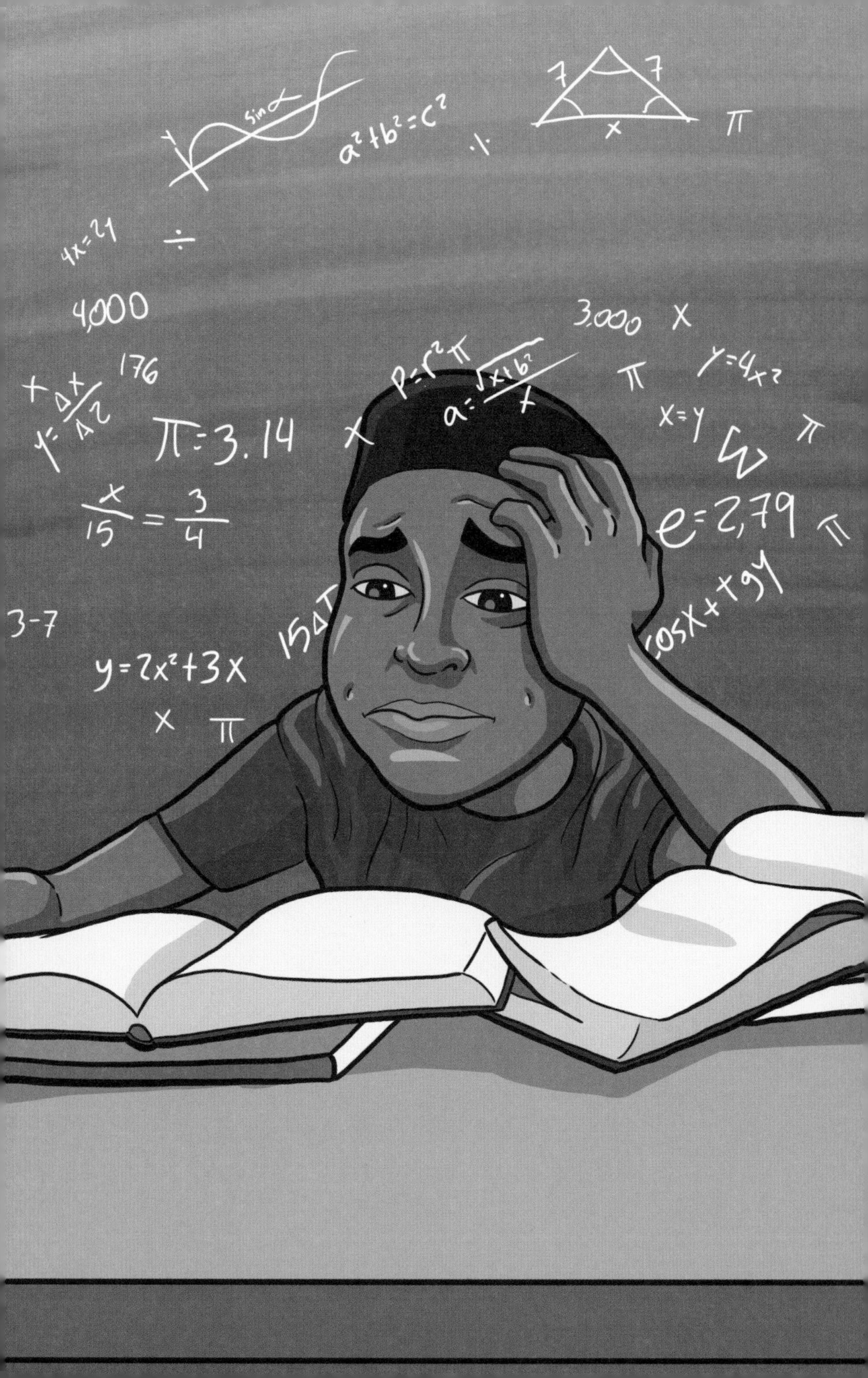

$a^2+b^2=c^2$
4,000
3,000 x
176
$y=4x^2$
$\pi=3.14$
x=y
$\frac{x}{15}=\frac{3}{4}$
e=2,79
3-7
$y=2x^2+3x$
cosx+tgy

Chapter 24

Asking for Help

Rule: It's Alright to Get Help

Peanut was getting good grades, but he started to have some problems in math again. He thought back to Mrs. Fry's class in California, when a failing grade got him a spanking. He wasn't failing Pre-Algebra, but he wanted to do better. He was irritated. Athletically, everything came easy to him. Academically, everything—especially math—didn't come easy at all.

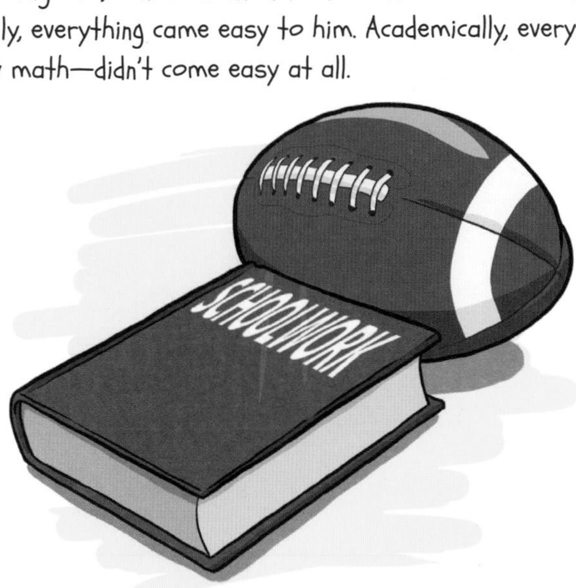
SCHOOLWORK

After class one day, Peanut approached Mrs. Moore's desk.

"I'm confused by some of this stuff," Peanut said. "Can you help me, Mrs. Moore?"

Mrs. Moore smiled.

"Absolutely, Charles," she said. "Why don't you meet me after school, and we can go over the lessons some more?"

During their sessions, Peanut appreciated Mrs. Moore's patience with him. She was always so calm. For 20 to 30 minutes, they'd walk through a few problems together.

Mrs. Moore tutored Peanut three or four days a week for nearly two months.

Peanut rushed to the mailbox on the day report cards were supposed to arrive at their home.

"Let me see; let me see!" Peanut said, grabbing the stack of envelopes.

He flipped through them, mostly bills and credit card applications.

Peanut eventually got to a yellow envelope. He knew his report card was inside. He ripped it open, and skipped over all the grades, looking for how he did in Pre-Algebra. He hoped his extra work with Mrs. Moore would pay off.

"A-. Great job, Peanut," Momma said.

Peanut was thrilled; his extra work with Mrs. Moore *had* paid off.

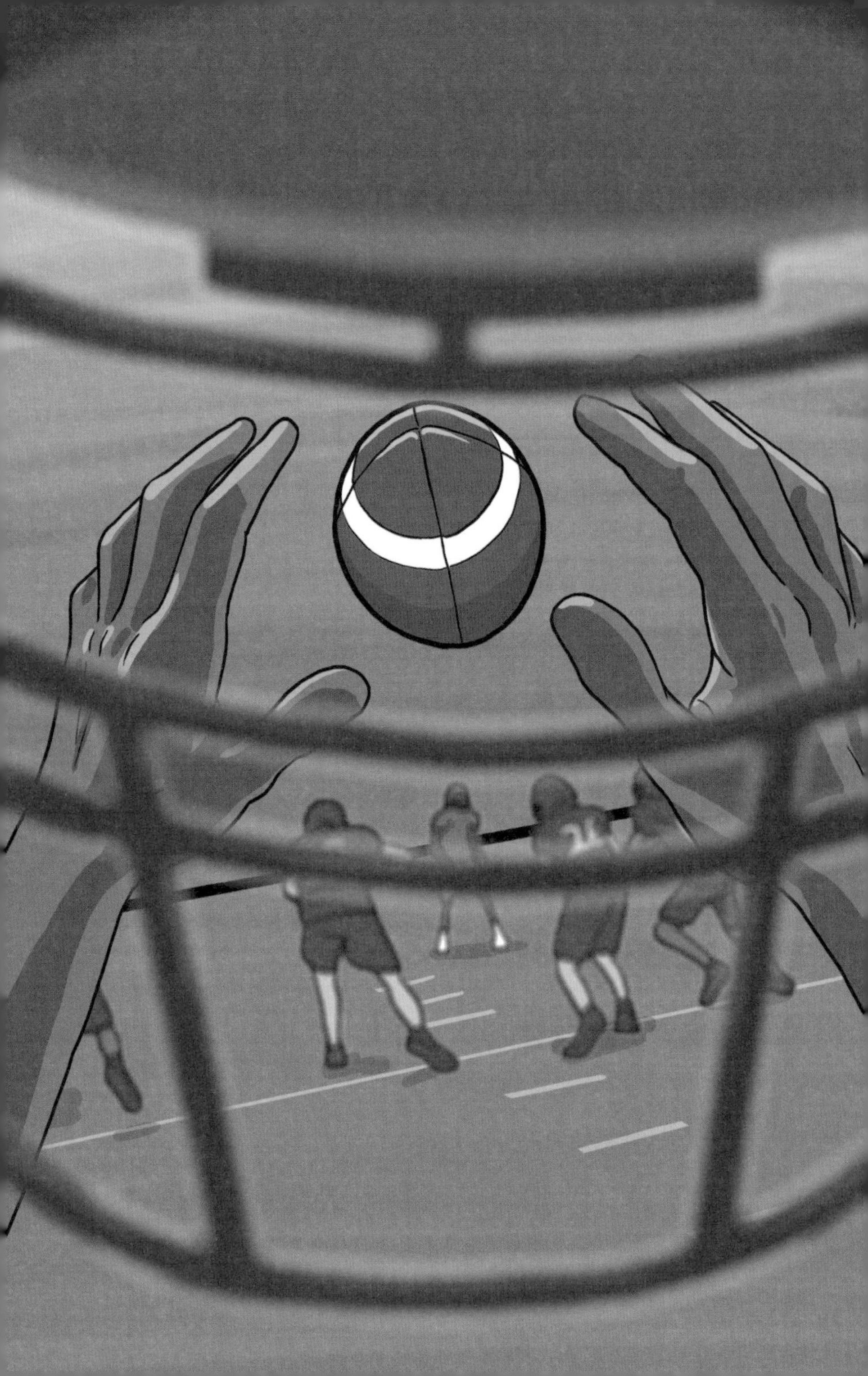

Chapter 25 The Best Player Plays

Peanut couldn't wait to start at Copperas Cove High School, especially to join the football program! The first step was to play on the Bulldawgs freshman football team, and he starred as a player and leader. Playing alongside many of his friends, Peanut helped the Bulldawgs freshman team finish the season without a single loss.

Heading into his sophomore season, Peanut would have a chance to make the varsity team. But he knew he had to get stronger.

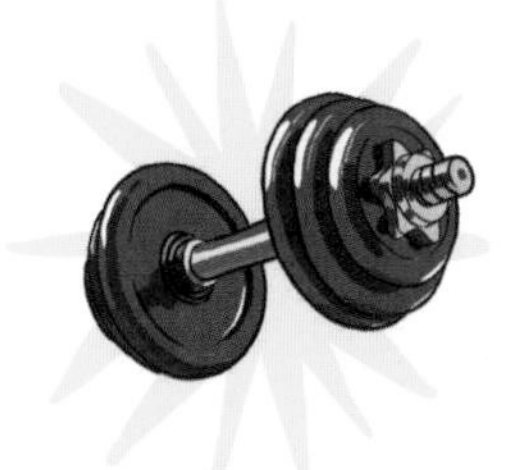

So Peanut and his best friend Jason Adams lifted weights five days a week during the summer, and they sprinted and practiced all the time. Though he didn't grow (Peanut was 5 feet 11 inches), he added 10 pounds of muscle and weighed in at 170 pounds.

If he was going to make the varsity team, Peanut would have to earn the starting free safety job ahead of senior Kevin Fagan. Kevin was tough. Kevin was smart. And Kevin had played well as the starter the previous season.

Peanut wasn't intimidated.

He felt even better when Coach Welch addressed the players before the start of two-a-days, when the team practices in the morning *and* afternoon.

"I want you all to know something," Coach Welch said. "I play favorites." He scanned the room, looking at his players.

"But here's the thing: You're *all* my favorites."

That led Coach Welch to one of his biggest rules:

Coach Welch's Rule

"The best player plays," Coach Welch said. "It's about the guy who gets the job done, no matter how old he is."

Peanut had excellent hands, and he could jump really, really high. Plus, he was an excellent listener, which impressed the varsity coaches.

Copperas Cove was a big school, with over 2,000 students. A sophomore hadn't started on the varsity team in a long, long time.

"Who should start at free safety?" Coach Welch asked his defensive coordinator, Rodney Southern.

"Well, I think it's pretty clear, Coach," Southern said. "It's gotta be Charles Tillman."

The next day, Peanut discovered he'd start at free safety *and* wide receiver.

"Wow," he told Jason. "I can't believe I did it."

In his first varsity game, against Austin Lanier High School, Peanut intercepted two passes in a 63–14 win!

In sports, Peanut had never felt more confident. His summer workouts with Jason had paid off, and he was helping the Bulldawgs on offense *and* defense. By season's end, he was named the district's best newcomer.

Peanut was used to being the new kid, but this was the first time he had ever been celebrated for it!

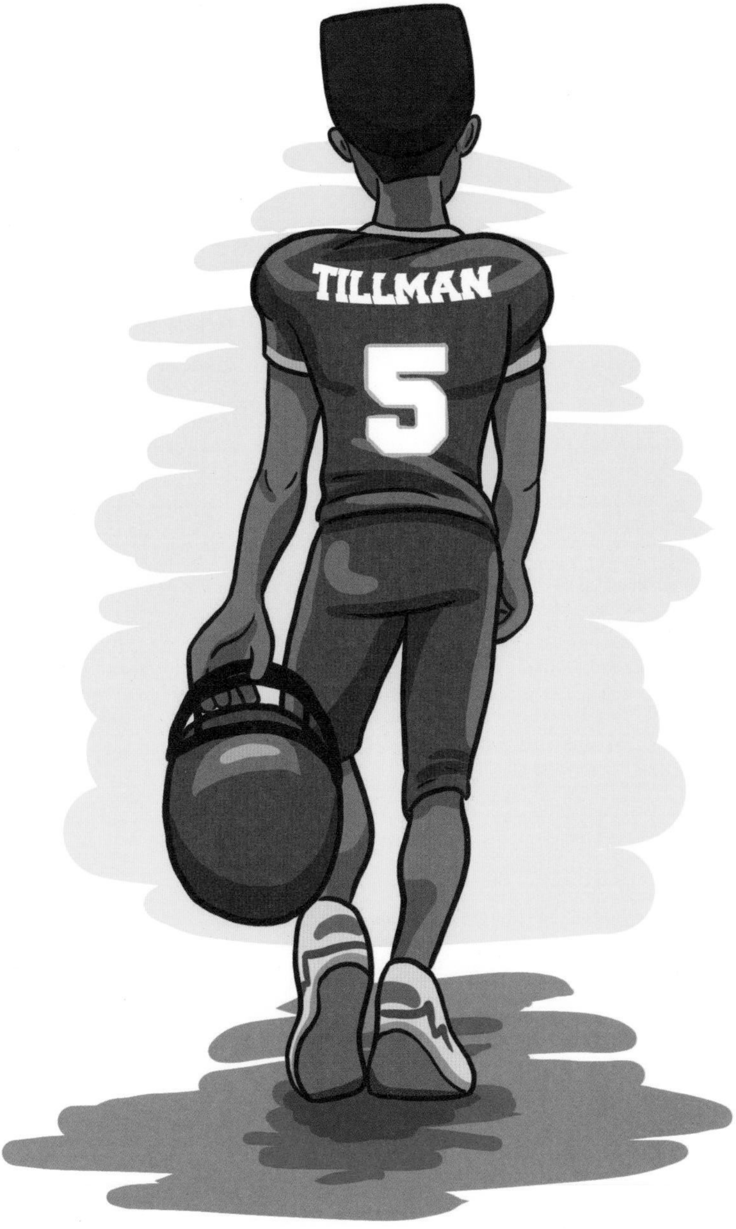
TILLMAN
5

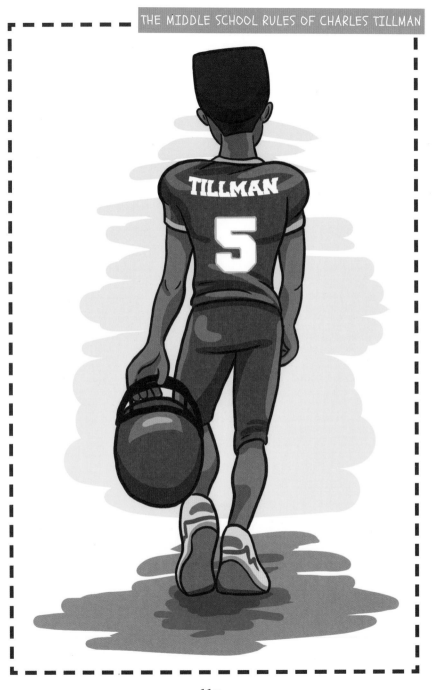

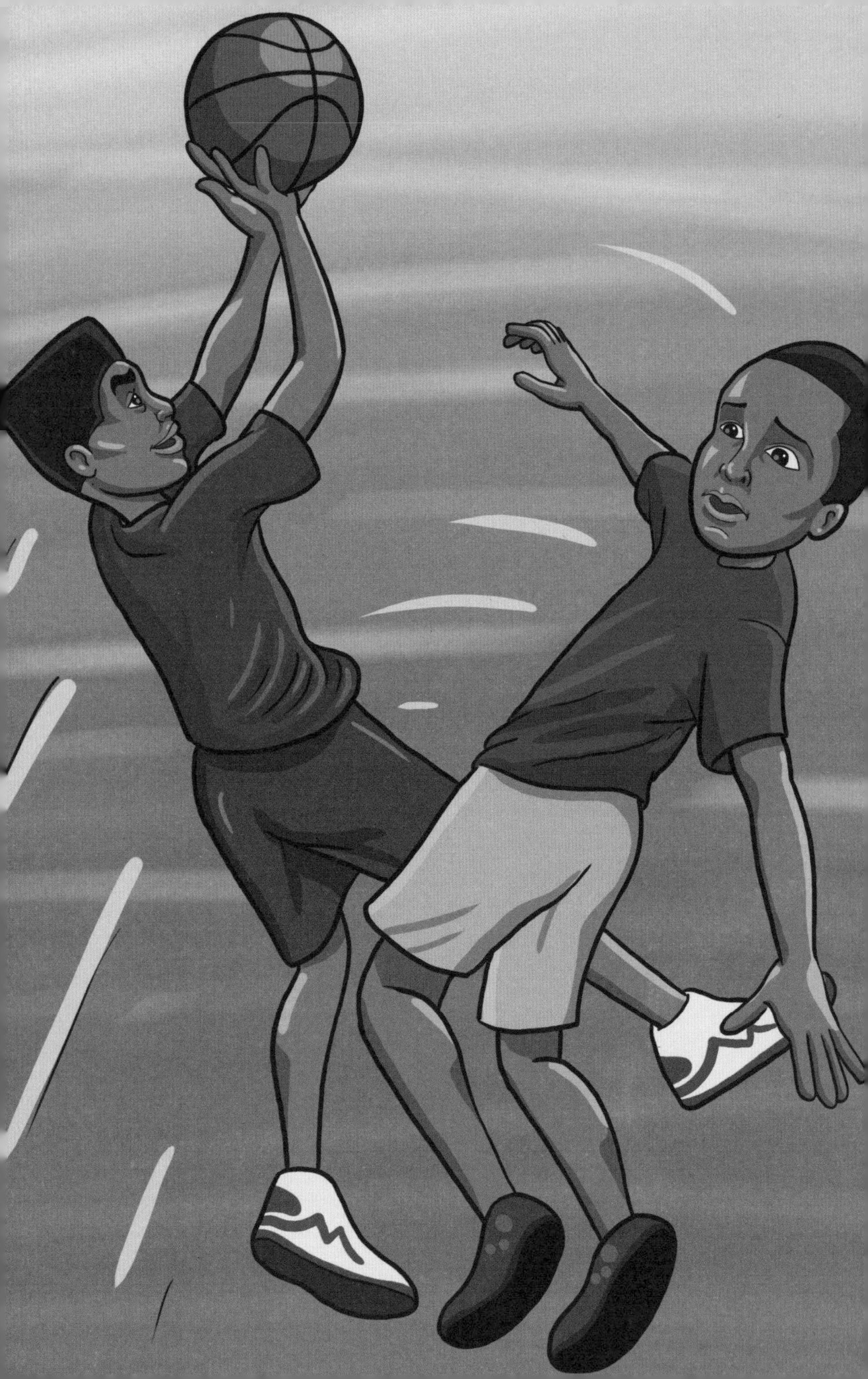

Chapter 26

A Long Time Coming

Rule: Be Persistent; Don't Give Up

After the family moved to Copperas Cove, Peanut and Duck weren't as close as they used to be; they both made their own set of friends. Right after school one day, on a side hoop at the high school gym, they decided to play a game of one-on-one.

"You know the drill," Duck said. "First one to 11."

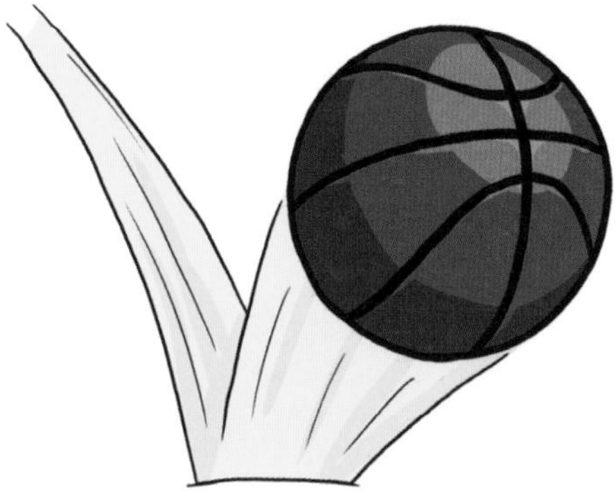

The brothers played hard, but they showed good sportsmanship. There were no free throws in one-on-one. But if the defensive player fouled the offensive player, then the offensive player would keep possession of the ball.

Duck jumped out to an 8–5 lead.

Don't give up, Peanut thought. *It's not over.*

Duck went cold for a few minutes—meaning he missed his shots. Peanut, meanwhile, got hot, nailing three jumpers in a row and making two layups. Peanut's five consecutive points gave him a 10–8 lead.

Duck wasn't about to give up though. He scored a reverse layup to make it a one-point game.

Peanut had the ball and the lead! *Will this be my big day to beat Duck?*

"Game point," he said. That meant he would win if he scored the final basket.

Peanut faked a jump shot from the top of the key, then he darted hard to his right toward the basket. Duck didn't bite. Peanut kept dribbling toward the basket.

Duck was in a good position close to the basket when Peanut stopped dribbling. He was sure Peanut wouldn't score over him. Duck was still bigger.

But after years and years, something had changed: Duck wasn't *stronger* than Peanut anymore. Peanut drove his hip into Duck's side, creating just a little space, and then jumped away from the basket. That move was called a *fadeaway*, and it was one of Michael Jordan's signature moves.

Before his two feet hit the ground, Peanut launched his shot, which hit the backboard... and splashed through the basket.

He won!

"Good game, Peanut," Duck said. "You finally got me."

Peanut had been playing and losing one-on-one games to Duck since he was seven years old. Sometimes, while he slept, he would dream of beating Duck in basketball.

Now I've made it, Peanut thought.

The time for dreaming was over. It was Peanut's time to shine.

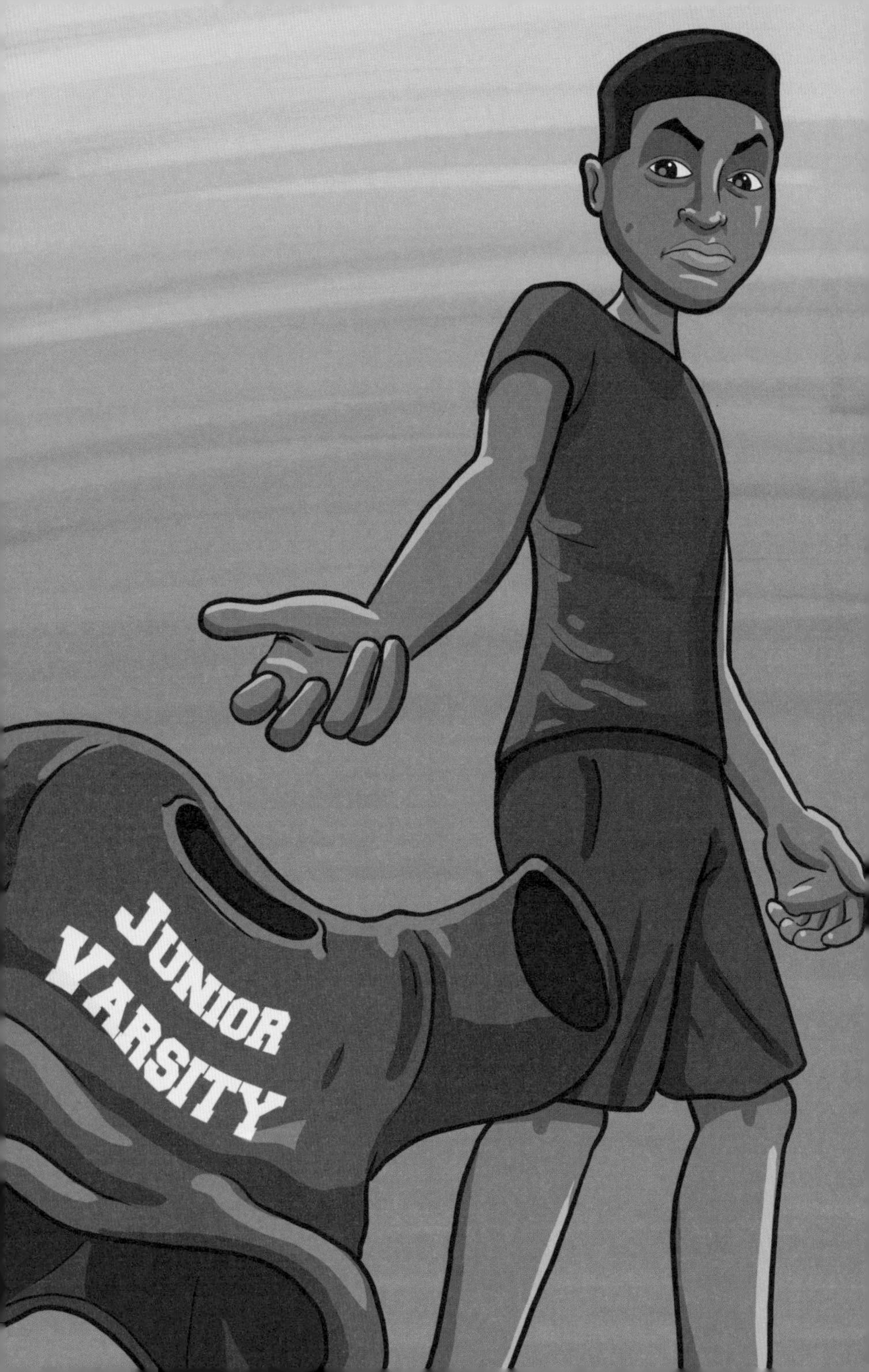
JUNIOR
VARSITY

Chapter 27

The "Demotion"

Rule: Be Humble and Patient

Everything was coming together for Peanut. He had defeated his brother in one-on-one, and he played varsity football as a sophomore.

Now I gotta make the varsity basketball team, Peanut thought.

Just as he did on the football field, Peanut proved to be one of his school's finest athletes. But on the basketball court, he wasn't one of the best shooters, passers, or dribblers.

When the varsity roster was announced, Peanut rushed to the door of the basketball coach's office. There were 12 names listed... and Peanut's name wasn't among them. He was on the junior varsity team.

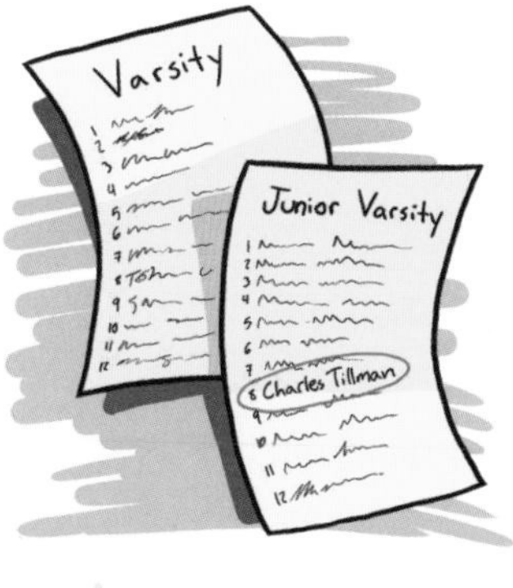
Varsity
Junior Varsity
Charles Tillman

Peanut was devastated. The junior varsity team played in front of small crowds, in hand-me-down uniforms, meaning their jerseys were not new. Peanut wasn't even starting on the JV team.

This stinks, he thought.

Because he was a varsity football player, Peanut figured he

THE "DEMOTION"

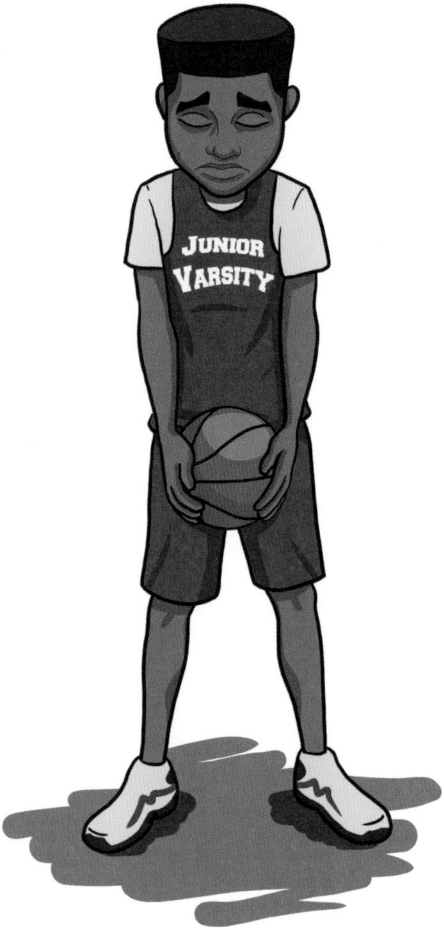

JUNIOR
VARSITY

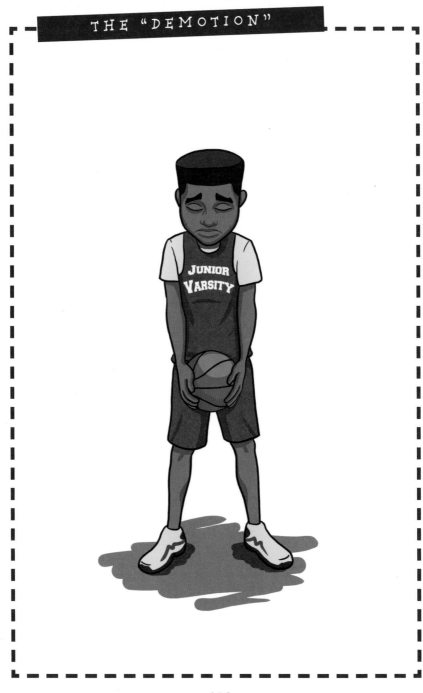

should play varsity basketball too. Being on the JV basketball team felt like a *demotion*. A demotion is a reduction in a person's role or rank. Peanut was too arrogant to recognize that he simply wasn't skilled enough to start on the JV basketball team, let alone play varsity. His attitude only worsened.

Over Christmas break, the Bulldawgs JV team was scheduled to play in a basketball tournament. Peanut decided not to go.

"This isn't for me," Peanut told Coach Ables.

"Are you sure?" Coach Ables asked.

"Yes I am," Peanut replied.

Peanut quit something for the first time ever. His parents would usually *intervene*—that means to step in and help. But Tiny and Lil' Donald were having their own problems.

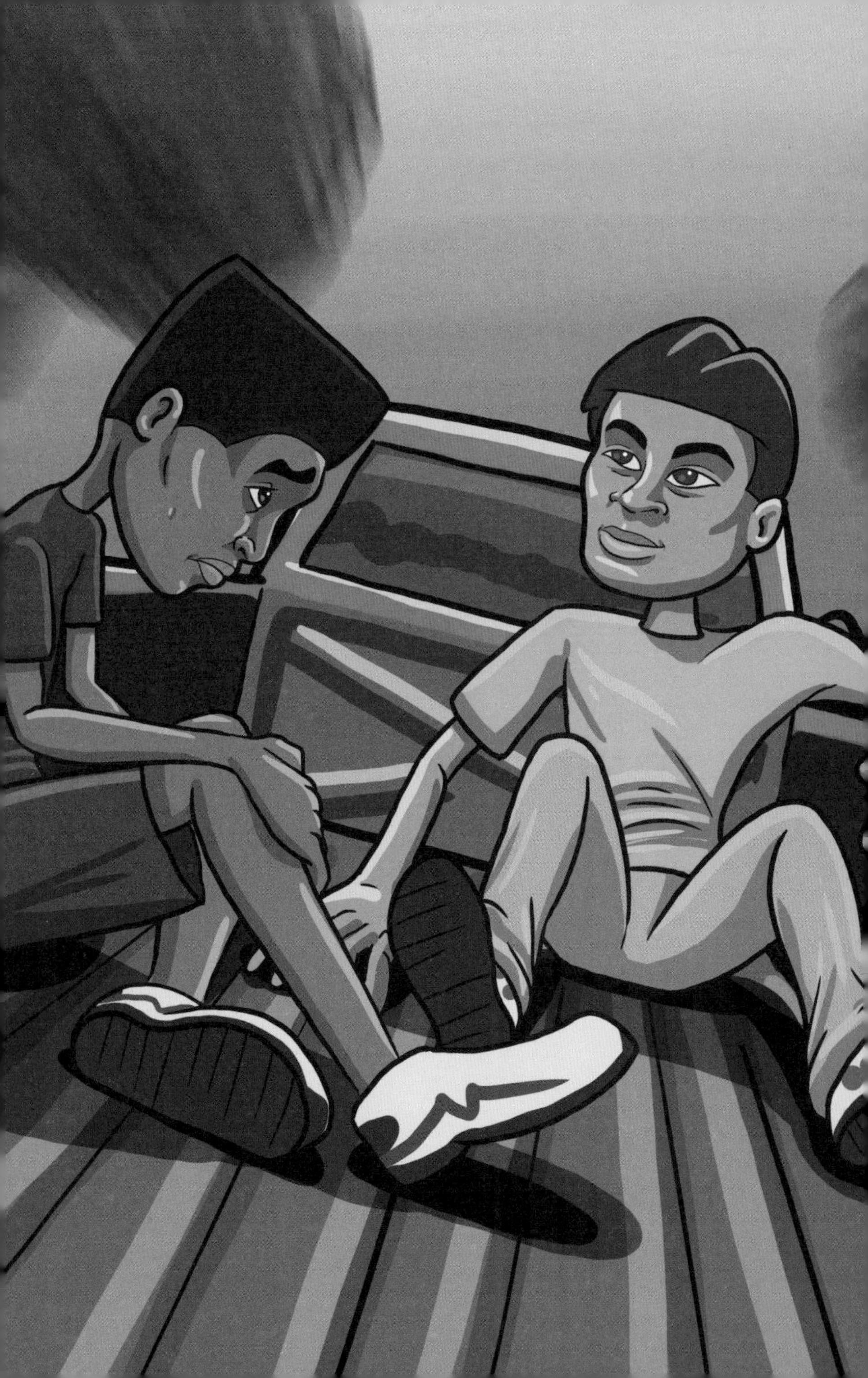

Chapter 28

Divorce

For the first time in his life, Peanut settled into a community... but his family started to drift apart. He had his sports, and Duck had his part-time jobs. Meanwhile, Tiny and Lil' Donald were arguing more and more.

Peanut would call his best friend, Jason, when Momma and Deddy started to have heated arguments.

"Hey, it's me," Peanut would say. "Can you come get me?"

Jason didn't need to hear any more. He knew Peanut wanted to get out of his house and stay with him. Jason's mom, Chun, sympathized with Peanut. Chun knew how hard it had been for Jason to see her and her husband go through a separation. So she never hesitated to make the 30-minute drive to pick Peanut up.

Chun had a small, 1990 Nissan truck, and Peanut and Jason would ride in the open cab, which didn't have seats. They would bounce around a little on the back roads, but they liked to be in the open air. Riding in the back of an open-cab pickup truck can be dangerous. In fact,

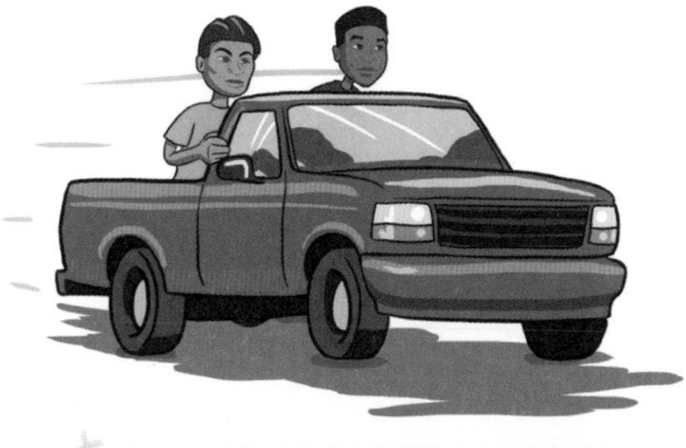

today, 30 states prohibit it.

Jason and Peanut had a lot in common. Their families were both from Chicago, and their parents both had failing marriages. Peanut trusted Jason, and he appreciated his friend's support.

For a few weeks, Peanut noticed Deddy wasn't around much. Then he came home and wanted to talk to Peanut and Duck. He had hard news and a painful lesson to deliver.

Deddy's Rule

"I'm never going to lie to you, even if it's something hard to say," Deddy said. "Your momma and I are getting a divorce, and I'm going to move out."

Peanut and Duck liked that Deddy talked to them like men, telling them the truth. But Deddy was right: the news was hard to say and hard to hear too.

Peanut's parents got a divorce, and Deddy moved into the barracks on the post. Momma was busy working. Peanut was often home alone.

Momma had always spoiled her sons, cleaning up their rooms, doing their laundry, and cooking their meals. But when Momma wasn't around, Peanut and Duck had to clean up their own messes and cook their own meals.

One night, Duck decided to make fried chicken and purchased everything from H.E.B.—a grocery store he worked at. He seasoned the chicken, and he heated up the oil in a big pot. There was only one problem: Duck had no idea how long to deep fry the chicken.

When the outside got nice and crispy, Duck pulled the chicken pieces out of the pot with tongs and placed them on a plate covered with paper towel. He fried up six pieces. When he cut one up, blood leaked out. Duck cut another piece, which also wasn't done. Eating uncooked chicken can make you very, very sick.

"Oh no!" Duck said to Peanut. "I didn't cook it long enough."

Peanut shrugged.

"What are we going to do?" he asked.

"Let's just go to Bush's Chicken," Duck replied.

Duck, who had a job, treated Peanut to dinner. Most nights, though, Peanut was on his own. If he wanted dinner, he had to make it himself.

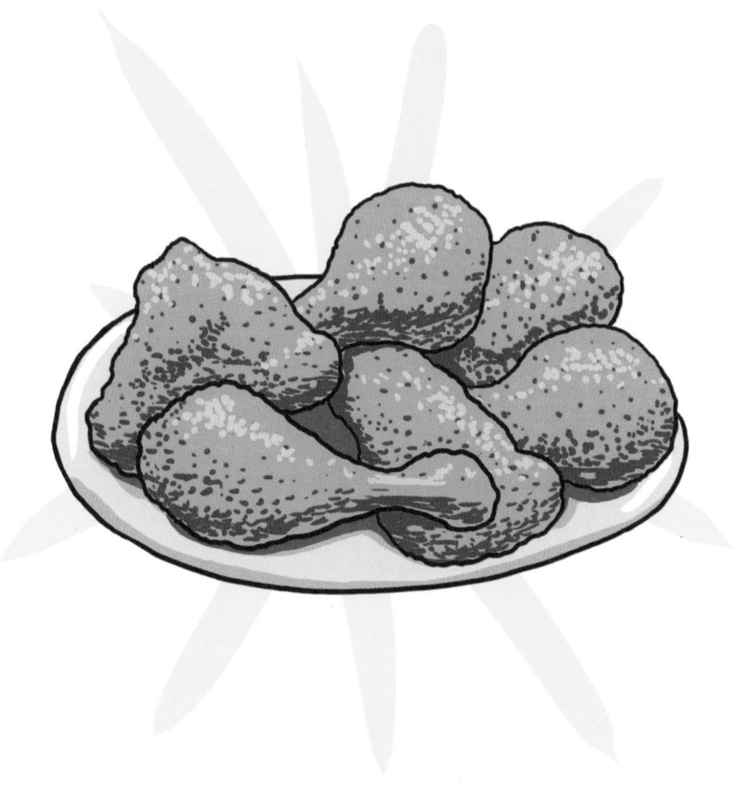